John Saul Howson

**The Metaphors of St. Paul**

John Saul Howson

**The Metaphors of St. Paul**

ISBN/EAN: 9783743418974

Manufactured in Europe, USA, Canada, Australia, Japa

Cover: Foto ©Lupo / pixelio.de

Manufactured and distributed by brebook publishing software (www.brebook.com)

John Saul Howson

**The Metaphors of St. Paul**

# THE METAPHORS OF ST PAUL

By JOHN S. HOWSON, D.D.
DEAN OF CHESTER.

STRAHAN & CO., PUBLISHERS
56 LUDGATE HILL, LONDON
1868

# CONTENTS

|     |                       | PAGE |
|-----|-----------------------|------|
| I.  | ROMAN SOLDIERS,       | 1    |
| II. | CLASSICAL ARCHITECTURE, | 40 |
| III.| ANCIENT AGRICULTURE,  | 87   |
| IV. | GREEK GAMES.          | 125  |

# I.

## ROMAN SOLDIERS.

EVERY part of Holy Scripture has its own distinctive imagery: and through the medium of this imagery its instruction is often conveyed. Thus, when we read the prophecies of Amos, "who was among the herdmen of Tekoa,"—himself a "herdman" in a wild and pastoral district,—the images are such as these: the fat "kine of Bashan, which say unto their masters, Bring and let us drink;" "the lion roaring in the forest;" "the seven stars of Orion, before the shadow of death is turned into the morning;" "the basket of summer fruit;" "the grasshoppers in the shooting up of the latter growth." Unless we rightly apprehend the circumstances, the scenery, and the pursuits, in connexion with which it was God's will that His prophet should speak, we cannot fully understand the meaning of His words; and so far, to us, their force and instructiveness is diminished.

The imagery of the Book of Amos is an emphatic and strongly marked instance of a principle which is applicable, in various degrees, to all parts of the Bible. The life of Joseph, the life of Moses, the life of Ruth, the life of Elijah, all have their appropriate atmosphere and colouring; and if we look at them without reference to these, they fade away into something abstract and dead. And so it is with the New Testament. But here, though the principle is the same, we feel that we are brought into a new world, and that the principle must be applied to very different details. Every part of the Old Testament has an oriental complexion. We illustrate it by referring to what travellers tell us of the tents of the Bedouin Arabs, of the courts of Eastern princes, of caravans and camels and palm-trees. And so it is, no doubt, to some extent, in the case of the New Testament. But still, on the whole, in passing from one to the other, we are conscious that a change has come over the scene, and that God has begun to speak to us now through similitudes of a different kind. We find ourselves brought in contact with circumstances far more nearly resembling those which surround us in modern life. We are in fact, when the New Testament is our study, on the borders or in the heart of Greek civilisation, and we are always in the midst of the Roman Empire. It is no more possible fully to understand what the Apostles say to us, than what the Prophets say to us, if we dissever their words from the circumstances of their lives. The metaphors they use are drawn (as indeed they must have been drawn, to be intelligible at all) from the things which were around them. My endeavour will be, in four sections, to illustrate certain groups of images which are common in one part of the New Testament, and, in the present section, while keeping in view especially one very notable passage in the Epistle to the Ephesians, to elucidate *the military metaphors of St Paul.*

It seldom occurs to us to consider how large a portion of his time St Paul spent in the close proximity of soldiers. He lived under the shadow of the greatest military monarchy which the world has seen. Englishmen are less able than others to realise all that is implied in this simple fact: hence they are startled into the impression of novelty, when they first travel in France or Austria, and see troops filing through the streets of every city, and large barracks in every country town. But such sights were no novelty to St Paul. No doubt they were more frequent and conspicuous in some parts of the Empire than others. In Philippi, for instance, in Troas, and the Pisidian Antioch, which were Roman

Colonies, we may well believe that the warlike symbols of Rome were more prominent than in other cities which he visited: and the state of Syria, which was a very uneasy province, and was held by a standing army of 60,000 men, was very different from that of Achaia or Bithynia, which were comparatively quiet and settled districts. But, wherever he resided, military uniforms and military quarters were familiar objects; wherever he travelled, he was liable to meet troops on their march from one province to another, or in the pursuit of banditti, or acting as an escort of prisoners.

But we are not left to this general kind of illustration. We are well acquainted with several incidents of his life, which connected him, in a manner peculiarly intimate, with Roman soldiers and their officers and their armour. It is enough to make a simple reference to his arrest in the court of the Temple, when the commandant of the garrison of Antonia, with some of his subalterns and a body of troops, ran down and took him into custody,—then to the time which the Apostle spent in the barracks within Antonia, and to the events which took place there,—then to his night journey to Antipatris, under the charge of a guard almost as numerous as half an English regiment, besides a squadron of dragoons,—then to his captivity of two years at Cæsarea, the centre of the provincial military government, where he was probably chained by the hand to a soldier,—then to his adventurous voyage, when an officer of a distinguished corps was his close companion, and when the swords of the soldiers under his command, which had cut the fastenings of the boat, were only just prevented from taking the Apostle's life and the lives of his fellow-prisoners,—then to the delivering up of the prisoners to the commander of the Prætorian Guards, after which, though Paul was suffered to dwell by himself, yet it was not without "a soldier who kept him,"— and lastly, to the facts hinted at in passages of the Epistles written at Rome, as when he says, in affixing his autograph to the Colossian letter, "the salutation by the hand of me Paul," and then, feeling the chain clank on his wrist as he writes, he adds, "remember my chains,"—or, in the Ephesian letter, when he describes himself as "an ambassador in bonds,"—an ambassador of the free Gospel, fastened to a soldier;—it is enough to enumerate these things, in order to see how natural it is that St Paul should speak to us in military metaphors, nay, how unnatural it would be (if I may say so with reverence) were no such metaphors to be found in his writings.

Our best mode of approaching the direct illustration of our selected context is first to notice some of those other texts where imagery of the same kind is more lightly touched by St Paul, and so to rise by successive steps to the allegory in which the Christian warrior is set before us in the full panoply of God. Then it will not be irrelevant if we turn in conclusion to some other passages, where similes from the same source are employed by the Apostle, less obviously but not less forcibly.

The first of these passages is in the thirteenth chapter of the Romans.* That Epistle was written at Corinth, which, both as the seat of local government, and because of its critical position on a strait between two seas, must have been garrisoned by a strong military force. The image which always rises before my mind when I read the passage, is this: I fancy St Paul—after a day spent in hard work, partly in tent-making and partly in preaching and in visitation among his converts—writing far through the night to the Christians in Rome, and just at daybreak, when the sentinels are changing guard, and the morning light glances on their armour,— while at the same time the last sounds of

* Rom. xiii. 11-13.

debauched revellers in the street fall upon his ears,—expressing himself in the now familiar words, "The night is far spent, the day is at hand; let us therefore cast off the works of darkness, and let us put on *the armour of light;* let us walk honestly, as in the day, not in rioting and drunkenness."

As to the phrase "armour of light," it is evidently equivalent to the phrase "*armour of righteousness*," which he uses elsewhere,\*— *i.e.*, spiritual armour for the contest against spiritual foes. But in the place where this last expression occurs, the idea is more fully developed than in the former case. Here it is "the armour of righteousness on the right hand and on the left." We have not simply

\* 2 Cor. vi. 7.

armour in the abstract, as in the other instance, but armour specially described as of two kinds, "*on the right hand and on the left,*"—*i.e.*, offensive and defensive, represented generally by the sword and the shield. St Paul is here describing himself, and his own attitude in regard to the resistance he had met with at Corinth in the progress of his apostolic work. This is not the only occasion in this severe Epistle (as we shall see afterwards) where he uses military language in describing his own position in reference to the enemies of the truth.

We reach something still more definite and specific, when we come to the fifth chapter of the first letter to the Thessalonians.* "We

---

\* 1 Thess. v. 5–8.

are not of the night . . . . therefore let us not sleep . . . They that be drunken, are drunken in the night . . . . Let us, who are of the day, be sober, putting on the breastplate of faith and love; and for an helmet, the hope of salvation." The chief remarks to be made here, I think, are that this Epistle was written from Corinth, like that to the Romans, but on a previous visit; that the whole context is very similar to that which has been quoted from the Romans; and that while this passage contains many more details than that just adduced from the second Corinthian Epistle, yet it is entirely limited to defensive armour. As to any observations on two pieces of armour that are specified, —" the *breastplate* of faith and love," and the "*helmet* of salvation,"—these belong more properly to our discussion of the allegory in the sixth of Ephesians,* which claims from us now a more direct consideration.

Enough has been quoted already to prove that the use of military metaphors is a familiar thing to St Paul. And in the passages hitherto adduced, these metaphors have one general type, which is quite in harmony with the longer extract before us. In examining its different parts, I should wish to be guided by the reverent belief that each word has a meaning,—that each word is the best that could be used,—and, at the same time, I should wish to be on my guard against that pedantry of interpretation which tortures the

* Eph. vi. 10–17.

Bible into meanings which it was never intended to bear, and which, in this case, would deprive the Apostle's imagery of all its freshness and elasticity.

I have called the passage an allegory. But it cannot strictly be described by that term. It is a series of images with a running explanation. In a pure allegory, the key of interpretation is to be derived from the context, or from the circumstances, or from analogy. But here the image and the interpretation are given side by side. We "wrestle" or engage in close conflict, but "not with flesh and blood," —*i.e.*, (as we see from a passage where the same phrase is used in the Galatians,) not with man, but with spiritual foes. We wear "armour," but it is the armour of light, the armour of righteousness, the panoply of God. We carry a "shield," but it is the shield of faith. We wield a "sword," but it is the sword of the Spirit. This is St Paul's manner. He explains his metaphors as he proceeds. We have, therefore, no need to waste our time discussing the principles of the interpretation of allegory. We may begin at once to go in order through the clauses of which the passage is composed.

One of the first thoughts which occur to us in looking at the introductory words is this, that the armour is of no use to us unless we put it on. We are not to be passive in the matter. The opening words give a positive injunction; and the only way to obey the injunction is to put on the armour, and to wear it and use it. Another obvious thought relates to the perilous condition of those who are destitute of this armour. Without it we are utterly defenceless. And it is no light matter to be defenceless in the presence of a foe, who is not only hostile, but accomplished in stratagem, and who commands an army such as that which is described in the verses before us. There is a story of a Spartan soldier, who went into battle without his armour, and who was fined by the Senate, though he had been victorious. This anecdote supplies a very useful admonition to the Christian soldier.

One word in this introductory portion is unfortunately translated in the Authorised Version. The phrase, "having done all," is by no means, in my opinion, an adequate rendering of the Greek. The marginal translation, "having *overcome*," is more correct. The original denotes that we are to beat down all opposition, and having done this, to "stand," to hold our ground. And this word "*stand*," which occurs once and again, sets before us the true nature of the Christian's conflict. We have a defensive military position to hold for God, and we must hold it. Our duty is no light skirmish, which might be half an amusement to those who enjoy a fray; but it is a serious and momentous struggle to hold the field where we are posted, like the struggle of those who fought at Inkermann.

I find in two of Chrysostom's sermons on

this chapter some remarks on these introductory verses, so good and forcible, that I think they deserve to be quoted. With reference to the wiles of the devil, he expresses himself as follows: "The Apostle saith not, Against the *fighting*, nor Against the *hostilities*, but Against the *wiles*. This enemy is at war with us, not simply, not openly, but by wiles: *i.e.*, he tries to deceive us, and to take us by artifice. He never proposes to us sins in their proper colours. Thus, he does not speak of idolatry, but he sets it off in another dress, making his discourse plausible, and employing disguises." In reference to the expression just alluded to, "having subdued all," he adds: "That is, having subdued our passions and vile lusts, and all things else that trouble us. The Apostle speaks not merely of doing the deed, but of completing it, so as not only to slay, but to stand after we have slain; for many who have gained this victory have failed again. *Having subdued all,* saith he, not, *Having subdued one and not another;* for even after the victory we must stand. An enemy may be struck, but things that are struck revive again." And once more, in reference to the word "stand," Chrysostom says: "The very first feature in tactics is to know how to stand well, and many things will depend upon that. In the case of mere athletic exercises, the word of command which the trainer gives before anything else is this, to stand firm. Much more will it be the first thing in military matters. The man who, in a true sense, stands, is upright; he stands not in a lazy attitude, not leaning upon anything. The luxurious man does not stand upright, but stoops; so does the lewd man, so does the lover of money."

This is enough concerning the *attitude and posture* of the Christian warrior. We come now to *the armour itself* which he wears. As described to us here, we observe that it consists of six pieces. A few words may be devoted to each of them. But first let us bear in mind how much reality and life are communicated to the description, when we recollect where St Paul was when he wrote it. He was in the midst of the Prætorian Guards, the *élite* of the Roman army, a body of men raised far more conspicuously above the legions than our Guards, or even the French Imperial Guard, are above the regiments of the line. But not only was he in the midst of them, seeing them continually, and hearing daily all the sounds of barrack life, but he was fastened to one of these guardsmen while he dictated the letter, and he felt the chain on his wrist while he affixed his signature.

First in order of enumeration we have the BELT — "having your loins girt about with *truth.*" By this we are not to understand a loose sword-belt, like that which our own officers wear, nor any ornamented girdle, but a very strong girding apparatus, made of leather, and covered with metal plates, and fastened firmly round the loins. The appearance and use of it are best seen in ancient statues in the British Museum and elsewhere. It was the first part of the armour which the soldier would put on, and it was of essential use to him for the purpose of safety, and especially for the sake of standing firmly. It was to the Roman soldier exactly what Truth is to the soldier of Christ. Of Christ Himself it is said in the prophecy, that "righteousness shall be the girdle of His loins, and faithfulness" (the word is *truth* in the Septuagint) "the girdle of His reins." \*

The BREASTPLATE is next to be considered. It is described as the "breastplate of *righteousness*." A question might be raised here as to the meaning of the word "righteousness," whether it denotes the justification which belongs to the believer by virtue of his union with Christ, or refers to that rectitude of character which cannot

Isaiah xi. 5.

be wanting in a true Christian. I feel little doubt that the latter is the true meaning of St Paul; and this for two or three reasons. In the first place, justification would seem to belong more naturally to the "shield of faith," which is mentioned below; but, again, it appears to me that all the parts of defensive armour mentioned here designate graces of Christian character. Moreover, in the shorter allegory of the first Thessalonian letter, the breastplate is described as made up of "faith and love," a perfect account of that principle in a Christian which leads him to feel rightly, to think rightly, and to act rightly; but hardly such a definition as we should expect of a sinner's state of pardon and acceptance with God. But there is another reason, which, to my mind, is almost decisive. St Paul is here again using Greek words from the Old Testament, (and it is important to observe this; for there is seldom any long passage in St Paul's writings without some quotation from the Septuagint,) and there we find it said of the Lord Himself, that "He put on righteousness as a breastplate, and an helmet of salvation on His head."* The incongruity is obvious on the former interpretation. "It is God that justifieth."

This reference to Isaiah leads me to break the order of St Paul's words, and to take "the helmet of *salvation*" next after the "breastplate of righteousness;" for they are coupled together in the same clause by the prophet from whom he quotes. Clearly we might have

* Isaiah lix. 17.

some difficulty here in assigning a precise meaning to the Christian's helmet, were it not that the Apostle himself comes to our assistance; for he says to the Thessalonians, that it is "the *hope* of salvation" which we are to take for a HELMET. I conceive, then, that we are to see here a representation of that cheerful and courageous hope which is so important an element in the Christian's warfare, and so bright an ornament and crowning point to all the other graces of his character.

The helmet is perhaps the brightest and most conspicuous part of a soldier's equipment; but there are other parts, less showy, but not less essential. A soldier badly shod can never last well though a campaign. Many of us have a vivid remembrance of what we read in the newspapers concerning some passages of the Crimean war. St Paul does not leave his description of the Christian warrior incomplete in this respect. "HAVE YOUR FEET SHOD," he says, "with *the preparation* (or with the prompt ready movement) *of the Gospel of peace.*" It is needless to enter here into any details concerning the military equipment of the feet, which enabled the Roman armies to march to the conquest of the world; but we should observe the holy irony with which St Paul gives an unexpected turn to his mention of this part of the Christian armour. The Roman soldiers were all on the alert in obeying orders to carry into every nation the miseries of *War.* The like alacrity ought to be shown by us in our obedience to our Captain; and no slip-shod indolence ought to make us slow in moving on this happy errand of *Peace*.

The words in which the Authorised Version introduces the SHIELD are again (I conceive) inadequate, or, at least, obscure. "Above all" conveys the impression of "especially," as though the Apostle were now about to mention what is most important. And perhaps "the shield of faith" is, in fact, the most important of all the defences of the Christian soldier. But I think the Greek words mean simply "over all," "on the outside of all." The great Roman shield referred to here was very different from the small bucklers which were used in some kinds of ancient warfare. Sculptured representations of it may be seen on Trajan's Column. It covered and protected the whole body; and whatever weak points there might be in other parts of the armour, this supplied their deficiencies, as faith comes to the rescue when all other graces are failing. True faith is invaluable and invulnerable. It is competent to quench even the "fiery arrows" of the Evil One. Here the image of the Christian conflict assumes all the animation of a *siege;* and one of the best illustrations I am acquainted with of the words used by the Apostle is in the history of one of the sieges of Rhodes, during which arrows charged with combustible materials were sent against the ships, and the very expression chosen here by St Paul is employed by Diodorus Siculus in describing the defences used for quenching the fire.

One part of the armour remains—THE SWORD

—"the sword of the Spirit, which is the Word of God,"—*i.e.*, the sword which the Spirit gives, and which is none other than God's revealed truth. This is the one offensive weapon. We are not sanctioned in the use of any other: all the rest of our armour is defensive: and this is very instructive. Our conflict is not with man, but with sin. We have no angry passions of our own to gratify. Our duty is stedfastly to resist: and when we strike, we must strike only with the weapon which God puts into our hands. All this is made more emphatic, if we observe that one weapon—the most characteristic weapon of the Roman soldier—the great *pilum* or pike, which Lord Macaulay has introduced with strict truth into one of his "Lays of Rome"—this weapon is entirely omitted. Here the parallel is left incomplete. Can we doubt that this was done purposely? The silence of Scripture has its meaning as well as its actual words.

I abstain from further and closer practical comments. These would enter into the region of Christian experience, and would belong to a treatise of a deeper kind. I will only now, through a few remaining paragraphs, follow the same thread of thought, where it conducts us to one or two other places, in which (as I have said) military metaphors are employed, less obviously at first sight, though not less forcibly.

Some of these relate to the long operation of *campaigning*, rather than the mere putting on of armour. Thus, when Timotheus is admonished to "endure hardness as a good soldier of

Jesus Christ," it is added by the Apostle: "No man that goeth on a campaign entangleth himself with the common affairs of life, that he may please him who hath chosen him to be a soldier."* It is to be regretted that the expression "*this* life" should have found a place in the English Version, inasmuch as it mixes the metaphor with the thing intended, besides stating what is not true. For if one thing above all others belongs peculiarly to this life, it is War. This, however, does not hinder war, in the form of a prolonged campaign, from furnishing most apt illustrations of three things which are expected from the Christian,—patient endurance,—firm separation from those interests which are not compatible with his main

* 2 Tim. ii. 3, 4.

purpose,—and an earnest desire to please his Commander.

There is again a passage in the early part of the second Epistle to the Corinthians,* which involves no difficulty as to its general meaning, but great part of the vividness of which we lose by not noticing how imagery, drawn from the conduct of a campaign, runs through the whole of the context. In the last passage the reference was to an individual soldier: here it is to a commander. St Paul is speaking in peremptory language of his apostolic power and authority. The military phraseology starts suddenly to view in the third verse—"Though we walk in the flesh, we do not war after the flesh." This is clear enough. But in what follows it is

* 2 Cor. x. 3-6.

not always remarked that every phrase to the end of the sixth verse is appropriate to some part of a campaign, and drawn in fact from the familiar experience of those terrible Roman wars which were well remembered in every region through which the Apostle travelled. No one will question this as regards the words "weapons," and "warfare." But the "strongholds" are the rock forts, such as those which once bristled along the coast of his native Cilicia, and of which he must often have heard, when his father told him how they were "pulled down" by the Romans in their wars against the pirates. Those "high things that exalt themselves"—those high eminences of the pride of nature—occupied in force by hostile troops,—had been a familiar experience in many wars throughout Asia Minor, while one of the grandest of all was the Acropolis that towered over Corinth. But this is not all. Ancient warfare ended with the taking of prisoners, who were carried into some safe place (such as this very Acropolis) where obedience would be secure. So the Apostle speaks of "bringing into captivity every thought to (or rather *into*) the obedience of Christ." And then, further, if in a country that had been conquered on the whole, rebellions were here and there to break out again, it was not the habit of the Romans to desist till complete subordination was established. So the Apostle holds himself in readiness to "revenge all disobedience," even when on the whole (for this he will not doubt) the general "obedience" of the Corinthian church is "fulfilled." Here then are a series of phrases which describe the vigorous prosecution of a campaign, and the determined subjugation of the last symptom of rebellion. And who will say that we do not lose by failing to notice this character of the language? Who will say that we do not gain by allowing it to have its natural and close association with what history tells of the course and the consolidation of Roman military conquest?

And more yet remains to be said concerning even this portion of the subject. St Paul pursues the progress of the campaign till it reaches that which, in a Roman's eyes, was the most glorious of all consummations—the progress of the triumphal procession after final victory; and he introduces God Himself as the victor and the leader of the triumph. Twice we find this image expressed, with the technical and classical word which belongs to the subject: once when the great conquest effected through the death of Christ is the topic of the Apostle's enthusiastic sentences,* and once when the progressive advance of the Gospel of Christ is represented in language strictly suitable to the long procession of conqueror and captives by the Sacred Way to the Capitol.† In the former case the words are brief and simple, which describe the "open display" of the defeat of "principalities and powers." In the latter the description is prolonged and given in detail. The doctrine preached by the Apostle "in every place" is compared to the fragrance which filled the

* Col. ii. 15. † 2 Cor. ii. 14–16.

streets from clouds of incense; while the fatal doom of the captives contrasted with the exulting joy of the citizens is a vivid representation of the awful alternative which separates the hearers of the Gospel into "them that are saved," and "them that perish."

And still the whole subject of the military metaphors of St Paul is not exhausted. There are other passages where the same expressive imagery occurs: as when he tells us that "without were *fightings,* within were fears," a description of his own experience which may well give encouragement to us :* or as when he speaks of the "law in our members *waging war* against the law of the mind and taking us captive;" and perhaps our own experience is enough to make us aware that no metaphor

* 2 Cor. vii. 5.

would be more suitable to the case than one derived from the dreadful realities of war :* or as when he assures his most consistent converts that "the *peace* of God, which passeth all understanding, shall *garrison* their hearts and minds through Christ Jesus."† This is an unexpected—almost an ironical—turn, like that which we noticed before, when we saw that "the preparation of the Gospel of peace" was an essential part of the "armour of God." And the natural conclusion of these remarks is an allusion to the Great Resurrection, when *"the trumpet shall sound,"*‡ and every faithful Christian warrior shall have his place in his own "order" or "*division*" of the vast Army of the Lord of Hosts.§

* Rom. vii. 23.
† Phil. iv. 7.
‡ 1 Cor. xv. 52; see xiv. 8.
§ 1 Cor. xv. 23.

# II.

## CLASSICAL ARCHITECTURE.

OUR last section was on the military metaphors of St Paul, with especial reference to the middle portion of the sixth chapter of the Epistle to the Ephesians. The present will deal with the *architectural metaphors* of the same Apostle, with prominent but not by any means exclusive reference to a passage in the third chapter of the ~~Second~~ [1st] Epistle to the Corinthians.

The thought which lies at the basis of these essays is this: that in order to understand an ancient writer it is not enough to study his books, but necessary also to know something of the fashion of his times,—not safe simply to work from the Dictionary, without some regard to the records of Monumental History,—without some effort to reproduce and realise manners and customs, and the outward expression of the old social life. Even in order to understand the bare meaning of the words, we must know something of the life. Much more, when we desire to appreciate the nicer shades of meaning, and to enter into the full force of illustrative language. For this purpose we have need of Archæology as much as of Philology. The two cannot prudently be dissevered. And more than this. Unless our Archæology is correct, — our Philology, being connected with anachronisms, will lead us into positive errors.

These observations, true of ancient writers in general, are quite as true of Sacred as Profane. Moses and Luke, Ezra and Paul, did not write independently of the circumstances with which they were surrounded, or of the tastes, pursuits, and habits of their time. If they had done so, they would have been unintelligible when they wrote. And they will only be approximately intelligible to us, unless we have the means of re-setting the words in their true associations. When a man has once seen a really Oriental city, and made himself familiar with the sights and smells of a bazaar, walked on the flat roofs, or stood among the camels, he has acquired a power of appreciating the Old Testament, such as no dead Lexicon could ever give him. And how great a help for the New Testament is gained,—when, in some good museum, a man has taken into his hand a silver Denarius, and looked at the fine features of Tiberius—worthy of a nobler character—and turned the coin round, and read the Latin inscription, and reflected on the possibility that this might have been the very piece of money that was shown to our Saviour, on the high probability that it was minted at the same time, and on the certainty that it was exactly like it, in size and material, in the "image and superscription!"

These are only superficial illustrations: but

they are illustrations of a principle :—and the application of the principle becomes important, exactly in proportion as the writer in question, whoever he may be, has some favourite classes of imagery drawn from the circumstances of his time,—and in proportion as those circumstances, from which the imagery is drawn, are in themselves peculiar and removed from the sphere of our own customary thoughts.

Now thus much may be said, without any danger of dispute, concerning St Paul's favourite illustrations, that they are drawn, not from the operations and uniform phenomena of the natural world, but from the activities and outward exhibition of human society, from the life of soldiers, the life of slaves, from the market, from <u>athletic exercises, from agriculture, from architecture.</u>

That there is a strong tendency to architectural metaphors in St Paul's Epistles no one will dispute. But it is worth while to remark that this tendency to refer to buildings may be observed not only there, but in his speeches too. Let us call to mind two speeches, uttered in busy centres of population, and in the midst of those who had glorious architectural works every day before their eyes. At Athens how grandly does the Apostle point mentally, if not literally, to the Parthenon and Propylæa and their associated statues on the Acropolis, telling his hearers that God, "seeing that He is Lord of heaven and earth, dwelleth not in *temples made with hands*," and that the Godhead is not "like unto gold, or silver, or *stone*, graven by art or man's device!"* And at Miletus how significantly and strongly does he conclude his address to those who had come from Ephesus, where Diana's temple was the most magnificent and prominent object,—"Now, brethren, I commend you to God, and to the word of His grace, which is able to *build you up!*"† How or why St Paul's style had this tendency it is needless to determine. It might be a matter of temperament or of education. He might have a taste for Architecture, natural or acquired. That he was a man of fine perceptions and strong social feelings cannot be doubted. And to such men it is natural to enter into the

\* Acts xvii. 24, 29; see verses 16 and 23.  † Acts xx. 32.

spirit of a great city and its outward expression as given in its buildings. Again we are told that Gamaliel, under whom the Apostle was instructed, was a man of enlarged mind, and by no means destitute of sympathy with the culture of the Greeks. However this may be, St Paul, writing under Divine inspiration, does use ideas drawn from buildings, as vehicles of instruction. Architectural phraseology is inwoven into the texture of his Epistles, and to a much larger extent than would at first sight be supposed.

Let us take, in the first place, in elucidation of this topic, a single word, the word "*edify*." This verb, or its substantive, "*edification*," occurs in some form or other about twenty times in the New Testament; and in every instance, except one, it is used by St Paul; and that exception is in the Acts of the Apostles,* a book written almost certainly under St Paul's superintendence. This fact is remarkable, and well adapted to arrest the attention. But it becomes still more marked, when we observe that, on proceeding to look for the Greek word of which "edify" is the English translation, (or rather the Latin translation, introduced from the Vulgate by Wycliffe,) we find that other passages must be added to the list, and all in the same Apostle's writings. To quote the places where "edify" and "edification" occur in the English would be needless. They are all ready in our memories for use when occasion requires. But, in order to transfer our

---

\* Acts ix. 31.

associations to the Greek word, which is actually St Paul's word, and to which they more properly belong, I may observe that the language is precisely the same when he lays down the principle of non-interference with another Apostle's work—" I will not build (edify) on another man's foundation;"\* that the same favourite image occurs when he expresses the utter inconsistency involved in a return from Christianity to Judaism—" If I proceed to build up the edifice which I took so much pains to pull down, I make myself a transgressor;"† and that, with regard to moral practice, he uses "build up" in a bad sense as well as a good one, when he says, after laying down the truth that it is Christian love which "builds up,"‡

\* Rom. xv. 20. † Gal. ii. 18. ‡ 1 Cor. viii. 1.

that if the strong brother approaches too near association with idolatry, the conscience of the weak brother may be " built up," * so as to eat that which is sacrificed to idols—may become, in fact, a structure of sin.  In this passage the Authorised Version has "edify" in the margin; and this is the word in Wycliffe's version.  The word is "build" in the other two passages which I have just quoted.  It is evident that even then the words "*edify*" and "*edification*" were narrowing themselves to their theological sense, while "*edifice*" has still continued to have its widest sense. Not that the narrowing process was completed for some considerable time.  Spenser uses "edify" in the sense of building; and I find it said of

* 1 Cor. viii. 10.

the Castle of Corfu in Hakluyt's travels, (under the date 1553,) "It is not only of situation the strongest I have seen, but also of *edification.*"

We might follow this disquisition on a single word into results of considerable interest.

The question has a bearing on *Christian Evidence.* It is something that the same prevalent metaphor is used, and in the same kind of way, in several of the Epistles which bear the name of St Paul. Unity of style tends to prove unity of authorship. If one man wrote all these Epistles, then all are authentic. So, again, it is always interesting to find a peculiarity which marks the Epistles marking also the speeches which are assigned to this Apostle in the Acts. It helps to prove that the Paul of the letters is the Paul of the narrative; and this, too, is something. Here it must in candour be added, that this argument, if applied to the Epistle to the Hebrews, tends to separate it from the Epistles which were undoubtedly written by St Paul. On some grounds, I am strongly inclined to believe that he did write the Hebrews; but this argument, so far as it goes, has a tendency the other way. In those passages, "He who hath builded the house hath more honour than the house: for every house is builded by some one; but He that built all things is God,"\*—and "a greater and more perfect tabernacle, not of this building" †—and again, "Abraham looked for a city which hath foundations, whose builder and

---

\* Heb. iii. 3, 4. † Heb. ix. 11.

maker is God"*—in these passages it is remarkable that the original words are quite different from those which are customary with St Paul when he speaks of building or edifying.

But again, the topic before us has a bearing on *Christian Doctrine*. I have an impression that we have acquired the habit of using the word "edify" in a way slightly different from that of St Paul, from whom we borrow it. We give it an individual application. We say that this or that—a book read in private—a sentence from a sermon—a providential occurrence—is edifying to the individual Christian, without reference to his social position in the Church. But "edify" with St Paul is always a social

* Heb. xi. 10.

word, having regard to the mutual improvement of members of the Church, and the growth of the whole body in faith and love. "The *Churches* in Judæa and Galilee and Samaria," it is said, "had rest and were edified."* Paul says to the Corinthian Church, "We do all things for your edifying."† He says to the members of the Thessalonian Church, "Edify one another."‡ And he tells the Ephesian Church that various ministrations are given, "for the edifying of the body of Christ§ .... from Whom the whole maketh increase of the body unto the edifying of itself in love."|| So, too, he says that Christians are, collectively as well as individually, the *Temple* of God. There are

---

\* Acts ix. 31.  † 2 Cor. xii. 19.  ‡ 1 Thess. v. 11.
§ Eph. iv. 12.  || Eph. iv. 16.

two passages,* one in the first and one in the second Epistle to the Corinthians, which may be instructively compared in reference to this point. Now, all this, if we consider the matter closely, is almost implied in the word, and in the metaphor which it represents. A building is an aggregate thing. And believers are not buildings, but parts of a building. St Peter calls them "living stones." I think we are sometimes too apt to forget this, and to treat Christianity (if I may use the expression) as if it were *monolithic*. We may lose in precision by not attending to the metaphors which are involved in Scripture words, and thus the proportions of our doctrine may be disturbed. It is not too much to say that, with regard to

* 1 Cor. vi. 19; 2 Cor. vi. 16.

the point before us, we might, out of St Paul's use of the word "edify" or "build," get a whole commentary on that article of the Creed—"I believe in the Holy Catholic Church."

However this may be, nearly all will agree that such passages as these have a very important bearing on *Christian Practice*. "All things may be lawful for me, but all things do not *edify*."* "We ought not to please ourselves, but let every one try to please his neighbour for his good unto *edification*."† "Let us follow after the things which make for peace, and things wherewith one may *edify* another."‡ The force of this last passage is much enhanced by the words which follow—"For the sake of meat do not run the risk of pulling to pieces the

* 1 Cor. x. 23.   † Rom. xv. 1, 2.   ‡ Rom. xiv. 19, 20.

work—the building—of God." The word here translated "destroy" in the English Version is not that which is so rendered a few verses above, ("For meat destroy not him for whom Christ died,") but it is the contrasted word opposed to "build," just as in that phrase, quoted before from another Epistle, (again an instance of the unity of St Paul's style,)—"If I build up again what once I pulled down" or "pulled to pieces." How vividly do we see this momentous duty of respecting scruples and prejudices, of forbearance in social intercourse, of controlling our vehemence and censoriousness, when we think of those around us as parts with ourselves of a building, which ought to be advancing in beauty and solidity! Those disorderly tempers disturb the proportion, that selfishness of ours mars the unity, those hasty words, those careless acts, are the pickaxes which loosen the mortar. And so with regard to public ministrations, "He that speaketh in a tongue, *buildeth up* himself: he that prophesieth, *buildeth up* the church" \*—"Forasmuch as ye are zealous of spiritual gifts, seek that ye may excel to the *building up* of the church," †—"Verily thou givest thanks well, but the other is not *built up*." ‡ If we neglect the principle involved in such a context as this—if we are bent on display and power and self-advancement — well may the Church be *dilapidated* instead of *built*. So, again, of the contrast of knowledge and love: "Knowledge inflates;" it only produces a bubble that will burst; but "love edifies"—it

---

\* 1 Cor. xiv. 3-5.   † 1 Cor. xiv. 12.   ‡ 1 Cor. xiv. 17.

constructs what is solid—its work is to be patiently building a noble and enduring palace.

But it is time that we advance from words to sentences. Let us examine a few passages where the architectural metaphor is more fully developed. We will follow a natural order, and take first the foundation, then the step, and then the furniture of the house.

We have seen that St Paul says he will not "build on another man's foundation," when he means to say that he will not trespass on another man's Missionary province. But he uses the same image in a deeper sense in various emphatic passages. In two of them there is the same juxtaposition of what is agricultural and what is architectural, which we have in this third chapter of the First Epistle to the Corinthians:

"Ye are God's husbandry, ye are God's building."* Just so, on turning to the Ephesians and Colossians, (again an illustration of the unity of authorship,) we find in one—"That ye, having your root and your *foundation* in love—your root as a tree, your foundation as a building †—may be able to know what is the love of Christ" —and in the other—"As ye have received Christ, so walk in Him, having your root struck down deep into Him and raising up the building on Him as your *foundation*."‡ A glance at the Greek shows that the language is the same in both passages. The only difference is, that in the former the Ephesians are addressed as having been set on a safe foundation, the Colossians are reminded of the duty of raising up the

* 1 Cor. iii. 9.   † Eph. iii. 17.   ‡ Col. ii. 6, 7.

structure so founded. Nor is this the only place in the Epistle to the Colossians where reference is made to the foundation.\*

But let us turn to two other passages, where the imagery is presented to us in detail. Both are good illustrations of what Paley calls St Paul's peculiarity of "going off at a word." In the nineteenth verse of the second chapter of the Ephesians, after he has happened to use the word "household," it seems as if the whole house rose before him, from foundation to roof, and transformed itself into a temple. The chapter concludes thus: "Ye are built upon the foundation of the apostles and prophets, Jesus Christ Himself being the chief corner-stone; in Whom all the building fitly framed together

---

\* See Col. i. 23.

groweth unto an holy temple in the Lord: in Whom ye also are builded together for an habitation of God through the Spirit."\* Now, all I will observe on this quotation is this: that I do not believe that the apostles and prophets are the foundation of which St Paul speaks; but that Jesus Christ is foundation-stone and corner-stone in one. I would render it thus: "Built on the apostolic and prophetic foundation-stone"—the stone which apostles and prophets laid, and on which they themselves rest—for "other foundation can no man lay, than that is laid,"—viz., Christ. The other passage is in the Second Epistle to Timothy. Having spoken of the overthrowing of the faith of some, the Apostle adds: "Nevertheless, the foundation of God

\* Eph. ii. 20-22.

standeth sure, having this seal, The Lord knoweth them that are His: and, Let every one that nameth the name of Christ depart from iniquity."\* What two grand inscriptions! Two eternal principles, one expressing the immutability of God, to drive away despair, the other describing the character of God's people, to drive away presumption. Well may they be indelibly cut on the apostolic and prophetic foundation.†

I said I would pass from the foundation to the step. The text to which I refer is again in one of the Pastoral Epistles:—"They that have used the office of a deacon well purchase to themselves a good degree."‡ This is an interesting passage, and I hardly think it is

\* 2 Tim. ii. 19.  † See Rev. xxi. 14.  ‡ 1 Tim. iii. 13.

to be understood as it is commonly explained. The English word "*degree*" is correctly used in the sense of *a step for further progress*, as it is used in Shakspere's "Julius Cæsar" of the climber up ambition's ladder:—

> "But when he once attains the utmost round,
> He then unto the ladder turns his back,
> Looks in the clouds, scorning *the base degrees*
> By which he did ascend."

I do not say that the words just quoted from St Paul are generally interpreted in the spirit of this speech of Brutus; but the popular interpretation involves some risk of taking this direction. I cannot but hesitate to believe that St Paul urges deacons to a discharge of duty either by the prospect of promotion, or by the charm of a higher position in the esteem of men. I should rather suppose that he alludes to their making sure of a firm spiritual standing, as before God and in prospect of the great day. This is more in harmony with the context. The "good degree" is coupled with "great boldness in the faith." All this they secure "to themselves." Besides doing service to the Church, they advance more and more in the confidence of their own spiritual life. With this expression it may be useful to compare what is said at the end of this Epistle (though there perhaps the metaphor is mixed) of the "laying up in store for ourselves a good foundation against the time to come, that we may lay hold on eternal life."\* And it is certainly a coincidence of some in-

---

\* 1 Tim. vi. 19.

terest that all the passages which I have just been adducing in reference to the foundation and basement of buildings, are from Epistles addressed to Ephesus—where that celebrated Temple was, on the substructions of which immense labour and expense had been lavished, that Temple which was full in sight when the mob cried out for two hours—"Great is Diana of the Ephesians."

But let us enter the house under the Apostle's guidance, and see what spiritual application he makes of the *furniture* which we find there. I follow the context of a passage which has already been partially quoted. In the Second Epistle to Timothy, in the second chapter, having described the foundation, he passes on to say :—" But in a great house there are not only vessels of gold and of silver, but also of wood and of earth; and some to honour and some to dishonour. If a man therefore purge himself from these, he shall be a vessel unto honour, sanctified, and meet for the master's use, and prepared unto every good work." * In the nineteenth verse he seems to set before us the Church in its essential character, as resting on an exclusive basis and marked by eternal principles: here, in what follows, the Church is exhibited to us in its mixed and outward character, lest erroneous conclusions should be drawn from the preceding. We have here a parable like the parable of the net: but we have something more than in the parable of the net. Not only are there two

* 2 Tim. ii. 20, 21.

classes — vessels of rich material to honour, and vessels of mean material to dishonour — but there are gradations in each class, gold and silver in the one, wood and earth in the other, not all among the good equally good, not all among the bad equally bad. A great house has a vast variety of furniture. In the twentieth verse we have the duty and the responsibility which arise from the consideration of this fact.

Our thoughts are carried, by natural association, from this passage to another of still more solemn import, where the same imagery is employed. I mean those verses in the ninth of the Romans, avowedly difficult even to the sternest Predestinarian, where the vessels of wrath are contrasted with the vessels of mercy

—the former fitted (not by God) to destruction, the latter expressly prepared (by God) unto glory.* I think we gain something, in the exposition of this passage, by following the line of St Paul's metaphorical language, and by putting the words in the Romans side by side with the other more explicit words addressed to Timothy. In that place we see that the Apostle does not urge his illustration beyond the point of contrast and classification. He does not say that because the furniture in a great house is separated into great classes, with subordinate gradations in each, therefore the members of the Church on earth are irrevocably so divided. He adds, that if a man keeps himself clear from association with the

* Rom. ix. 21-23.

meaner vessels, he will himself become one of the nobler. So in the Romans we have the two classes set before us; the sure tendency of the one to destruction, unless there is a recovery; the great truth that the glorious condition of the other is due to God only. All else is left open and untouched. The language is not so much argumentative as illustrative. It is of great importance, in the interpretation of Scripture, not to press a metaphor beyond the point which it was intended to elucidate, and not to deal with allegory as though it were logic.

Now, in drawing towards the conclusion of this section, I wish to revert to a remark which I made at the outset, viz., that a careful notice of the significance of imagery is all the more incumbent on us, in proportion as the circumstances from which that imagery is drawn may be peculiar. We ought to keep in mind the distinctive character of Classical Architecture, and to remember that it was from *this* architecture that St Paul drew his illustrations. We are apt to give too Oriental a colouring to the New Testament, and this for an obvious reason. The Classical world has passed away. We must reproduce it, if we wish to see it as it was. But, to realise the outward circumstances of the Old Testament, we need only read the books of travellers, and study the pictures of modern artists. We see Abraham in every sheik; Rebecca is at the well near every village; the climate and the seasons are in the main unaltered. But the colonial lictors at Philippi, the Prætorium at

Rome, Pilate with his official chair on the piece of tesselated pavement—these must be reinstated in the scene, if we are to see them at all. The materials for reproducing the life exist in abundance in literature and museums, but the life itself does not exist; and the work of reproducing it requires the union of exact scholarship rightly applied, with a lively imagination under the control of judgment. Now, the illustrations which St Paul connects with human habitations are not drawn from the wilderness—not from the transient dwellings of nomadic life, but from the solid cities of the Greeks and Romans. We might quote, in elucidation of this, a verse where he uses that very contrast to heighten the emphasis which he wishes to give to a forcible passage: "I know that if this earthly dwelling, which is only a tent, is taken to pieces, I have a *building* of God, a house not made with hands, eternal in the heavens."\* Nor is it from any Eastern kind of architecture, but from Classical architecture, that St Paul draws his metaphors of this class. There is one passage which might at first sight be thought an exception; but it is not really such. I allude to that place in the Ephesians where he says that Christ has "broken down the middle wall of partition, that He might reconcile both Jews and Gentiles unto God in one body."† I imagine there is a tacit reference to that partition wall in the Jewish Temple, on which notices were put up, forbidding Gentiles to enter the inner court. But then Herod's Temple was of

\* 2 Cor. v. 1. † Eph. ii. 14, 16.

Classical architecture, like the great structures in Athens and Ephesus—not, as Solomon's may have been, of some eastern Phœnician style, like the buildings of Tyre. Josephus gives us a full description of the Corinthian columns. Even the notices on the partition wall were in Latin and Greek. The complexion of Palestine in St Paul's day was probably European rather than Asiatic; and we should be quite in error if we were to imagine the monotony of a modern Eastern town to be the type of what he habitually saw in Cæsarea, or even in Jerusalem.

Now, are there any peculiarities of Classical Architecture which we ought to take into account when we comment on any of the illustrations which, for our instruction, St Paul was inspired to draw from that source? It seems to me that there are two. One is this, that all conspicuous Greek buildings, and most of the conspicuous Roman buildings, of his time, were characterised by vertical columns, supporting a horizontal entablature.

The significant application of this peculiarity is seen at once in that passage, where, in a time of controversy, he adduces the support of James and Cephas and John, who had the recognised reputation of being " pillars " in the Church.* Here the Church is evidently treated as a building—a palace, or temple, or the like ; and these three men are spoken of, not simply as stones in the building, just as ordinary Christians might be, but as characteristic and essential parts—as both ornaments and supports.† Now,

* Gal. ii. 9. † See Rev. iii. 12.

apply this to another context, concerning which some dispute has almost always existed: "These things I write, that thou mayest know how thou oughtest to behave thyself in the house of God, which is the Church of the living God, the pillar and ground of the truth."* I hold it to be an indefensible distortion of the passage, from polemical reasons, to take these last words and connect them with what follows, thus: "The pillar and ground of the truth, and without controversy great, is the mystery of godliness." I see no reason why the Church should not be called a pillar and support of the truth. What, indeed, would become of the light without the candlestick? But I am very much disposed, notwithstanding, to think that this is

* 1 Tim. iii. 14, 15.

not the meaning of the passage. I am inclined to believe that Paul says this to Timothy: "I write to thee, seeing that thou hast a prominent and responsible place in the house of God, in order that thou mayest fill that place aright, and be thyself indeed a pillar and support of the truth." In favour of this view, we have the analogy of the passage just adduced from the Galatians. We have also this consideration, that the Church is a building, not a pillar, while a pillar is a partial support of a classical building, and one ornament out of many. It is in the criticism of just such a passage as this that I would claim for Archæology its right to be combined with Philology. Not that there is any grammatical objection to the interpretation I am advocating; nor is the sanction wanting of early commentators, whose instinctive sense in a case of this kind is of considerable moment.

The other architectural feature of ancient cities, to which I desire to invite attention, brings us at once to the passage from that third chapter of the First Epistle to the Corinthians, to which reference was made at the outset. I believe that in such cities as Ephesus, where the letter was written, or Corinth, to which it was addressed, there was a signal difference (far greater than in modern European cities) between the gorgeous splendour of the great public buildings, and the meanness and squalor of those streets where the poor and profligate resided. The former were constructed of marble and granite; the capitals of their columns and their roofs were richly decorated with silver and gold; the latter were mean structures, run up with boards for walls, with straw in the interstices, and thatch on the top. This is the contrast on which St Paul seizes—slabs and pillars of marble and granite, and gold and silver, on one hand—wood, hay, stubble, on the other—to set forth two very different results of the spiritual edification (I use the word in its neutral sense) which goes on in the Church. Sometimes the passage is treated as though the picture presented were that of a dunghill of straw and sticks, with jewels, such as diamonds and emeralds, among the rubbish. But such an image would be utterly improbable in itself, and out of harmony with all the context. The whole allegory is strictly and consistently architectural.*

* See pp. 126–129.

In order to enter into the full significance of the allegory, we should look at the context. St Paul is addressing those who were addicted to the spirit of party, and is speaking of the right estimate of Christian Ministers. He first uses an agricultural metaphor, and then he passes to an architectural. Our approach to the architectural structure lies, as it were, through a garden or orchard. Here Paul has planted the precious trees. Apollos, and probably others with him, as subordinates and successors to Paul, are watering them. Suddenly the image changes to a new one, more capable of being turned to what the Apostle wishes to enforce. A building in progress rises before us. Paul has laid the foundation—laid it once for all, and laid it well. He has no objection to say this, for it has been done by the grace of God. On this foundation Apollos and others are building. As to building on another foundation, this is set aside at once. The work is going on, and will go on indefinitely in the future; but it will be tested. A day will come when the fire will burn up those wretched edifices of wood and straw, and leave unharmed in their glorious beauty those that were raised of marble and granite, and decorated with silver and gold. The men who raised such structures as these shall not only be safe, but rewarded; the men who lost their time on the others shall just escape out of the conflagration, because they built on the right foundation, but their escape shall be barely an escape.

It is a most serious admonition to the Minister of the Gospel "to take heed how he buildeth," that is, with what materials—what kind of teaching, what kind of parochial arrangements, what kind of provision for the young, what kind of care for tender consciences or for desperate guilt. He should consider, too, what his materials have cost him. If they are cheap and worthless, the first that came to hand, what fate can he expect for his building in the day of trial? Is it not well worth his while to see that the quarry is worked for the stone, and the mine explored deep for the silver and the gold, that all his materials may be precious, solid, and good, and may survive the fire, as the temples of Corinth itself survived the conflagration of Mummius, which burnt the hovels around?

It will be gathered that I think the building

itself in this passage is not simply the development of doctrine and the promotion of sound practical truth. These I look on as the materials of building. The building itself I should regard, in analogy with all that has preceded, as the *persons*, or rather I ought to say the *characters*, which result from this good or bad edification.

But still the passage may be lawfully applied to remind us of the importance of regular and systematic instruction in religious truth. And hence a lesson may be drawn, which has reference to the responsibility of the recipients, not the givers, of instruction. And we may conclude with an extract from the first of the Catechetical Lectures of St Cyril, which he delivered about the year 347 A.D. in the grand

Basilica erected by Constantine the Great: "Abide thou in the Catechisings," he says. "Though our discourse be long, let not thy mind be wearied out. For thou art receiving thine armour against the antagonist power: against heresies, against Jews, and Samaritans, and Gentiles. Thou hast many enemies. Take to thee many darts." He uses here the military imagery, which was the subject of the first of these essays. Presently he uses the agricultural imagery, which will be the subject of the next of the series. "Study the things that are spoken, and keep them for ever,—considering this to be the planting season. Unless we dig, and that deeply, how shall that afterwards be planted rightly, which has once been planted ill?" And then—quite in St Paul's own manner—he passes to the simile with the consideration of which we have been occupied in the present essay:—"Or consider Catechising to be a kind of building. Unless we dig deep, and lay the foundation,—unless by successive fastenings in the masonry we bind the framework of the house together, that no opening be detected, nor the work be left unsound, nought avails all our former labour. But stone must succeed stone in course, and corner must follow corner, and, inequalities being smoothed away, the masonry must rise regular. In like manner, we are bringing to thee stones, as it were, of knowledge. Thou must hear concerning the living God; concerning the Judgment; concerning Christ; concerning the Resurrection: and many things are made to follow one the other, which, though now dropped one by one, at length are presented in harmonious connexion. But if thou wilt not connect them into one whole, and remember what is first, and what is second, the builder indeed buildeth, but the building will be unstable."

## III.

## ANCIENT AGRICULTURE.

RAPID transitions from one metaphor to another are characteristic of St Paul.

One transition of this kind is to be found in the eighth verse of the tenth chapter of the Second Epistle to the Corinthians. St Paul has been using language drawn from the incidents of a campaign to describe the course which he himself might be forced to adopt, if those to whom he writes, or others, were to persist in their disobedience. In such a case he might be compelled to put all his spiritual power into action, and to "pull down" their "strongholds" of arrogance and pride, just as the rock-forts of his native Cilicia were destroyed in the Roman wars with the pirates. Such a course of procedure would be a cause of deep regret to him: for, as he says in the verse before us, the "authority" which "the Lord had given," was intended for purposes of "edification" or building up, not for purposes of "destruction" or pulling down. This is the last echo of the military image,—or rather not the very last echo,—for the identical phrase is found again at the very close of the Epistle,*— but it *is* an echo of the military image, though

---

\* See 2 Cor. xiii. 10.

in the English version it is muffled, as it were, so as to be almost inaudible: and the fact to which attention is invited is the close juxtaposition in one sentence of the military and the architectural metaphor.

Another instance of rapid transition may introduce us directly to the subject of the present section. The *agricultural* metaphors of St Paul are not by any means the most prominent, but they constitute a sufficient topic for one essay. "Ye are God's husbandry, ye are God's building," he says to the Corinthians, in the ninth verse of the third chapter of his First Epistle. The agricultural and the architectural image are here side by side, as, in the last case, the architectural and the military. We have already given our attention to the architectural allegory which follows this point of transition. Our subject now is the agricultural allegory which precedes it. "I have planted, Apollos watered; but God gave the increase. So then neither is he that planteth any thing, neither he that watereth: but God that giveth the increase. Now he that planteth and he that watereth are one: and every man shall receive his own reward according to his own labour. For we are labourers together with God: ye are God's husbandry."\*

Paley points out very acutely the delicate yet perfectly unconscious harmony of this passage with what we read in the Acts, and uses it as an argument for the authenticity of both the Epistle and the History. Not only must Paul

\* 1 Cor. iii. 6–9.

have been at Corinth before Apollos, but Apollos must have been there in the interval between the Apostle's visit and the writing of this letter. This is not our subject now, except so far as this, that it leads us to mark more closely the Providential sequence of one teacher after another in God's gracious work of preparing and maturing His Church.

This image of a large cultivated garden, in which many are employed, is indeed a most apt, a most copious illustration of nearly all the main characteristics of the Christian Ministry. There is first the succession of which I have spoken,—the tasks assigned now to one and now to another, according to the law of the seasons and the will of the great Master of the garden—one beginning when another has left off—one completing what another has prepared. At the same time there is justice to each: "Every man shall receive his own reward according to his own labour." And yet all the work is one. Though many hands are employed, according to their aptitude and the time when they are required, the progress is one through the advancing year to one result: "He that planteth and he that watereth are one." All, too, is entirely dependent on an unseen power: "Neither is he that planteth any thing, neither he that watereth: but God that giveth the increase." Then there are the lessons of cheerfulness, hopefulness, and patience—the habit of not looking for immediate results—but at the same time the confident expectation that in spite of adverse weather the flower and fruit will come at last—which all are necessarily associated with the very thought of a garden, and which should be diligently fostered by every Christian Minister in his own heart and mind. And lastly, there is the duty of giving diligent heed to the young plants. How much may be expected, if they are vigilantly and carefully tended at first, one by one! "Let us get up early to the vineyards; let us see if the vine flourish, whether the tender grape appear, and the pomegranates bud forth."\*

It has been said before, that the references to nature in St Paul's writings are almost entirely to nature in connexion with human labour; not to its beauty and to the impressions which the mind passively receives from it, but to its useful

\* Cant. vii. 12.

and beneficent processes under the work of cultivation. There is hardly any mere natural imagery in his Epistles. We find more of this kind of illustration in the one short Epistle of St James, than in all the writings of St Paul. What we read in the fifteenth chapter of the first letter to the Corinthians :—" There is one glory of the sun, and another glory of the moon, and another glory of the stars : for one star differeth from another star in glory,"*—is no real exception to this. This is not an outburst of adoring admiration, like those of the Psalmist " when he considered the heavens, the work of God's fingers, the moon and the stars, which He had ordained." † It is really the continuance of the preceding argument, and a new illustra-

---

\* 1 Cor. xv. 41. † Ps. viii. 3.

tion arising out of that which he had used before. He had been speaking of the difference between "bodies terrestrial," or the organisation of beings like ourselves adapted to an existence on earth; and "bodies celestial," or the organisation of beings, like the angels, adapted to a heavenly residence. And nothing is more natural (if I may so speak) than that this contrast should suggest another connected with the heavens themselves. The sun, the moon, and the stars, though they all give light, are very different among themselves, and each is suited to its own place and its own function. So above he had said that among the organisms of animal life on the earth there are great varieties, each according to its office in the economy of God's world: "All flesh is not the same flesh;

but there is one kind of flesh of men, another flesh of beasts, another of fishes, and another of birds." Now, going backwards again along the line of the Apostle's illustrations, we have the passage which I am aiming at: "But some man will say, How are the dead raised up? and with what body do they come? Thou fool, that which thou sowest is not quickened except it die: and that which thou sowest, thou sowest not that body that shall be, but bare grain, it may chance of wheat, or of some other grain: but God giveth it a body as it hath pleased Him, and to every seed his own body."* Here we have that reference to nature in its connexion with human labour and its productive operations rather than its mere phenomena, to which allu-

* 1 Cor. xv. 35-38.

sion was made just now. As, in speaking to the uneducated Lystrians, St Paul had urged "the rains from heaven and the fruitful seasons" as an argument for gratitude and a lesson against idolatry, so here he presses on the speculative Corinthians the facts with which they were familiar in the sowing and reaping of every year, as one reason for casting aside all theoretical objections to a resurrection of the body. The grain and the corn-plant, the seed and the harvest, are the same, and yet not the same. They are so connected as to be identical, and yet a wonderful change of form and organisation has taken place under the operation of mysterious laws. Why should it be otherwise with our own frames? He returns to this illustration again, after deviating just rapidly to touch the other illustrations: "So also is the resurrection of the dead. It is sown in corruption, it is raised in incorruption: it is sown in dishonour, it is raised in glory: it is sown in weakness, it is raised in power: it is sown a natural body, it is raised a spiritual body. There is a natural body, and there is a spiritual body."* We have here, then, what I think may truly be termed an agricultural allegory. The appeal is to the universal experience of man in the work of husbandry. And if there is just one Jewish touch where the subject is first approached in this chapter—"Christ the first-fruits, afterwards they that are Christ's at His coming"—this is quite what we should expect. †

This image of the harvest, in various applica-

---

\* 1 Cor. xv. 42-44.  † 1 Cor. xv. 20, 23.

tions, as we know, pervades the whole of Scripture, from its very earliest portions, from the dreams of Joseph or of Pharaoh, and the gleaning of Ruth and her mother. But St Paul uses it so pointedly, and so much in a way of his own, that I think it may be included as an element in his characteristic style. The progressive change of organisation, along with absolute identity of being, has just been adduced as a type of the Resurrection. How solemnly is this thought (in the sixth chapter of the Galatians) connected with the ultimate results to ourselves in eternity of the life which we lead in the moments of our time! "Be not deceived; God is not mocked: for whatsoever a man soweth, that shall he also reap. For he that soweth to his flesh shall of the flesh reap corruption;

but he that soweth to the Spirit shall of the Spirit reap life everlasting."* Here is the principle of inevitable retribution, the growing and growing, according to irresistible laws; the moral organism passing into new forms without losing its identity, just as the rich waving harvest is developed from the poor shrivelled grain. And clearly here the human side of the subject, the actual agricultural process, is a very prominent part of the image and the lesson, whether it be viewed in the aspect of warning or of encouragement. And the same train of thought meets us in a nearly contemporary Epistle, in reference to another subject,—namely the blessing, "twice blest," of generous giving. "He which soweth sparingly shall reap also spar-

* Gal. vi. 7, 8.

ingly: and he which soweth bountifully shall reap also bountifully;" "God loveth a cheerful giver." It is written of such a man that he "disperses abroad—he gives to the poor"—and yet he is no loser—his "righteousness"—or rather it ought to be, his liberality and beneficence, his power of doing good—"endureth" still.* A man is no loser by sowing his grain, in faith, with an open hand; he secures the harvest, and he secures a larger supply of grain than ever, for sowing in future over wider fields. In the encouraging verses which conclude the passage, I will not stay to inquire whether the true reading gives the Apostle's words in the form of a promise or a prayer; for indeed promises and prayers in the Apostolic writings run into

* 2 Cor. ix. 6–9.

one another, so that we can hardly distinguish them, even as the readings of the manuscripts do in such passages. "Now He that ministereth seed to the sower" in the world of nature and in the work of agriculture—"may He multiply (or, He shall multiply) your seed sown, and increase the fruits of your righteousness,"—or rather, as before, "your liberality and beneficence,"—"being enriched in everything unto all bountifulness, which causeth through us thanksgiving to God."\* No imagery could set before us more vividly the rich and increasing reward which waits upon faithful and generous service on our side, or the overflowing blessing on God's side, which gives life and abundance and growth to all honest spiritual husbandry.

\* 2 Cor. ix. 10, 11.

This passage leads me to single out a word which is certainly very characteristic of St Paul. The word "*riches*" has often been noticed as marking his style; and the same is true of the word "*fruit;*" and not merely is this a verbal, but also a moral characteristic. It seems to me to express that kind of exuberance, so to speak, which will never allow him to hope and believe by halves. The former word is a metaphor from the market, the latter from the corn-field or the orchard. He desires to visit the Romans, that he may "have some *fruit* among them also, as among other Gentiles."\* Writing to the Philippians of the precariousness of his life, he says (so I understand him) that he valued this continuance "in the flesh" as the condition

\* Rom. i. 13.

of bringing forth "*fruit*" in his work.\* Writing to the Colossians, his expression concerning the Gospel is, that in all the world it is ever "growing," and ever "bringing forth *fruit.*"† And this I notice (unless I am mistaken) as a mark of St Paul's way of using this word, that he always applies it to what is *good*. And that this should be so seems to us very appropriate and very beautiful. The blessedness of the righteous man is that, planted as he is "by the waterside," he "bringeth forth his fruit in due season," whereas the ungodly is "like the chaff which the wind driveth away."‡ The passage which most naturally occurs to us here is that in the Galatians where the *fruit* of the Spirit is contrasted in detail with the *works* of the flesh.§

\* Phil. i. 22.    † Col. i. 6.    ‡ Ps. i. 3, 4.    § Gal. v. 19-23.

It is a contrast very similar to that which we find elsewhere between the *wages* of sin and the *gift* of God.\* Nor is that passage in the Galatians a solitary instance. We find the same in the Ephesians—" Walk as children of the light; for the *fruit* of light is in all goodness and righteousness and truth,"†—the force of which is very much enhanced by our observing what follows: " Have no fellowship with the *unfruitful* works of darkness." And similar language is found in the Epistle to the Romans—"What *fruit* had ye then in those things whereof ye are now ashamed?" but " now, being emancipated" from that dreadful master, sin, and " become servants to God, ye have your *fruit* unto holiness, and the end everlasting life."‡

---

\* See Rom. vi. 23.  † Eph. v. 8, 9, 11.  ‡ Rom. vi. 21, 22.

Sometimes the phrase is applied generally, as (not to repeat again that passage concerning "the *fruits* of righteousness" addressed to the Corinthians)\* when he desires that the Philippians may be "filled" with those "*fruits* of righteousness which are by Jesus Christ to the glory and praise of God,"† or that the Colossians may be "*fruitful* in every good work, and increase in the knowledge of God."‡ Sometimes the reference is specific, as when he says that he is going to Jerusalem to deliver and lay up safely in store, and to seal, "the *fruit*" of the liberality of the Christians in Macedonia and Achaia;§ or when he says afterwards of similar generosity which came to himself from

---

\* 2 Cor. ix. 10. † Phil. i. 11.
‡ Col. i. 10. § Rom. xv. 28.

Macedonia, "Not because I desire a gift; but I desire *fruit* that may abound to your account;"\* or when he urges in one of the Pastoral Epistles that they who profess Christ's religion must learn to maintain good works, and contribute to those wants of others which must of necessity be brought before them, in order that with all this profession they "be not *unfruitful.*" † But in all these cases, whether they are general or specific, the reference is to what is good. One apparent exception may very naturally here come into the mind, namely, that passage in which two consecutive verses end, the former with the phrase "bring forth *fruit* unto God," the latter with the phrase "bring forth *fruit* unto death."‡ But these verses occur in the seventh of the Ro-

---

\* Phil. iv. 17.     † Tit. iii. 14.     ‡ Rom. vii. 4, 5.

mans, and even if the image were the same, I think it would be natural to call the passage an oxymoron, and so it would really be an instance of the rule, and not an exception. I conceive, however, that the image is different, and that the reference is to fruit as the offspring of marriage. I believe it will be found true, that when St Paul applies to moral subjects the word "fruit," as derived from the corn-field or the orchard, he applies it to what is good. I say nothing of the other parts of Scripture. But it is as if he thought the term too honourable—expressing as it does the result of man's honest, useful labour, in subordination to and in dependence on the bounteous and life-giving influences of heaven—too honourable and too cheerful to be applied to what is bad. "The root of the righteous yieldeth fruit."\* "He shall be as a tree planted by the waters, neither shall cease from yielding fruit." †

One particular passage—a remarkable and difficult passage—in that Epistle to the Romans, now claims a moment of close attention.‡ I allude, of course, to the allegory drawn in the eleventh chapter from the grafting of the olive-tree. The image first appears in the sixteenth verse, and (as we have seen in other instances) in close combination with another image—"If the first-fruit be holy, the lump is also holy; and if the root be holy, so are the branches;" and then it is rapidly developed with varied and pointed application up to the end of the twenty-fourth verse. With all the great doctrinal and

\* Prov. xii. 12. † Jer. xvii. 8. ‡ Rom. xi. 16–24.

historical questions arising from this passage, we have on the present occasion nothing to do; our concern is with the outward imagery, and in it there is this very strange circumstance, that the lesson is drawn from the grafting of branches of a wild olive-tree on the stock of a good olive-tree—the grafting of branches of a wild fruit-tree on the stock of a good fruit-tree—a process unheard of among gardeners. Commentators have tortured themselves with this difficulty, and some of them have adduced instances of this process with certain supposed good results as regards the productiveness of the olive. I confess I am very sceptical on this point, and the explanation which I suggest is very simple, though I am not aware of having seen it previously suggested elsewhere. I believe that here partly is the very point of the parable, that the grafting *was* contrary to the law of nature. So strange a grafting as that which had taken place in the case of the Gentiles made the lesson far more emphatic to them. It was the very *contrary* to the grafting which took place in the olive-grounds to which all readers of the Epistle were accustomed. This work of artificial cultivation is indeed the basis of the parable, but it is the basis by way of contrast rather than of comparison. So our Lord, in St Luke's Gospel, compares God to a *selfish* man and an *unjust* judge, and makes the argument for the answering of prayer all the stronger.* Or let us take another illustration. St James says to the rich tyrants of his day, "Your gold and silver is rusted, and

* See Luke xi. 8, xviii. 6.

the rust of them shall be a witness against you."* Now gold does not rust. St James was quite aware of this. But herein, I apprehend, is one part of the point of the image. Their very gold should become mysteriously their curse. So in the case before us. St Paul knew very well the processes which took place in the olive-grounds which were abundant then, as they are now, in all parts of the Levant. He must have seen them often when he was a boy at Tarsus. Boys notice all such things; and the experience of early life becomes, even in an Apostle, the basis of religious teaching. To find fault with him for inexactness, seems to me very like finding fault with him (as some critics do in these days) for inaccurate applications of the Old Testa-

* James v. 3.

ment. He knew the Old Testament, and so did his Jewish readers, far better than we do. But we must not leave our proper subject.

And one other side of the subject must be touched before it has been handled completely. Agriculture has to do with the animal as well as the vegetable world; and something within this province, too, in the writings of St Paul, will reward our careful attention.

I have sometimes been impressed with the fact, while thinking of this topic, that the critical words addressed to the Apostle from heaven at the threshold of his Christian career, were in truth *an agricultural metaphor*—"Saul! Saul! it is hard for thee"—Who knows—I write it with reverence—whether at that moment the operations of ploughing might not be going on within sight of the road along which the persecutor was travelling? At all events, the image is certainly drawn from those operations, as certainly as the images in the Sermon on the Mount were drawn from the lilies which grew in the field, or the birds which flew over it. All who have journeyed in the East, or even in the south of Europe, are familiar with that ox-goad, the resistance to which only increases the suffering of the restive animal, and in allusion to which the force of conscience, sharpened by God's Spirit, is depicted in the words, "It is hard for thee to kick against the pricks."* And it seems to me interesting to notice, on the one hand, that our blessed Lord's words spoken on this occasion from heaven were a parable, like the

* Acts xxvi. 14.

parables which He graciously uttered on earth, and, on the other hand, that they are in harmony with, and might almost be fancied to have given a holy suggestion of, one class of the Apostle's own habitual imagery.

I may remark that what was said in the earlier part of this section in reference to orchards, vineyards, and corn-fields, has its counterpart here in reference to flocks and oxen. St Paul's illustrative language deals with human labour and its useful results, rather than with nature viewed poetically on the side of beauty and mere expressiveness. Accordingly, the animals under the care of man are presented to us more on the industrial side than the contemplative. It is the farmer near the large town, rather than the shepherd in the wilderness, who comes before us in the pages of this Apostle. It is remarkable that nowhere, in all his unquestioned Epistles,* is Jesus Christ set forth as the Good Shepherd. I do not forget those touching words in the address at Miletus, "Take heed to the flock; feed the church which God hath purchased with His own blood; for grievous wolves shall enter in, not sparing the flock." † And perhaps it would be strange if no one instance were found in St Paul of the employment of an image which is almost universal throughout the rest of Scripture. But still it is not characteristic of his style. It is very different with regard to St Peter, in whose first Epistle these words, "Feed the flock; be examples to the flock," ‡ are a true echo of the words at the end of

* See Heb. xiii 20.  † Acts xx. 28, 29.  ‡ 1 Pet. v. 2, 3.

the Gospels, "Feed my sheep, feed my lambs."*

With St Paul's habit of illustration the concourse of men, where business goes on and buying and selling, is more in harmony than the solitary mountain-side, where the sheep are following their shepherd and diligently cropping the thin herbage on the rocky slopes. We see this in that passage of his Epistles when he does mention the *flock*. "Who goeth a warfare any time at his own charges? who planteth a vineyard, and eateth not of the fruit thereof? or who feedeth a flock, and eateth not of the milk of the flock?"† the real meaning of which is this, "Who keeps a vineyard or a flock of sheep without living by the profits of the grapes and

* John xxi. 15–17.  † 1 Cor. ix. 7.

the milk, when they are brought into the market?" In this case, as in so many others, three metaphors—one military and two agricultural—are rapidly thrown together. The point on which they are brought to bear is the claim which Christian Ministers have on the support of the people, whether or not they may find it necessary or politic to urge that claim. With this it seems natural to combine another passage in another Epistle (remarkable also for the heaping up of metaphors), though there the duty of the *minister* to *labour* among his people is urged, his support being assumed, while here it is *their* duty to *support* him which is pressed, his labour being assumed. "No man that enters on a soldier's career mixes himself up with the common business of life; no man, striving in the games, will obtain the prize unless he has kept the rules; the husbandman that laboureth must be first partaker of the fruits;"* *i.e.*, it is the farmer that works who has *the first claim* to the profits of the produce of the farm. The idle Farmer, the idle Clergyman, deserves to starve. Perhaps the word "fruits" might more naturally seem to connect this sentence with the earlier part of this section; but it is better to have taken it in its present connexion, because of the common bearing of both these passages on one subject—the Christian Ministry—which also is the subject of the one remaining passage with which I am now about to conclude.

"Thou shalt not muzzle the mouth of the ox that treadeth out the corn." When a sentence

* 2 Tim. ii. 4–6.

from the Old Testament is more than once quoted in the New Testament, it always seems to have a peculiar claim on our reverent attention. And St Paul quotes this sentence from Deuteronomy* twice, in two Epistles written at very different periods, and each time brings it to bear on the same topic. "It is written in the law of Moses, Thou shalt not muzzle the mouth of the ox that treadeth out the corn. Doth God take care for oxen? or saith He it altogether for our sakes? For our sakes, no doubt, this is written: that he that plougheth should plough in the hope of a harvest, and he that thresheth should do this in the hope of partaking of the harvest," † (for so I conceive the true meaning of the latter words would be given.) The eye

* Deut. xxv. 4.   † 1 Cor. ix. 9, 10.

ranges here over the whole agricultural process, from the ploughing and sowing to the reaping and threshing, and all this ought to be conducted in hope; otherwise all the cheerfulness, all the elasticity of the work is gone. The Christian people ought to be very careful that their Clergy are not weighed down by the perpetual harassing care of the maintenance of their families and the education of their children. When they see all the harvest of wealth around them, they ought, if they labour patiently, at least to have some small share of it. There may possibly, as Chrysostom says, be a hint to them—to this effect, that they do labour diligently, that they be not impatient under the irksome monotony of routine, and that they be content with, it may be, a very scanty portion of all this profusion of wealth. But the main lesson is to the Christian people, that they support the hearts and the strength of their Clergy by endowments, and gifts, and liberal payments, and still more by sympathy, and respect, and large co-operation. The lesson is riveted for ever on the Church, in strong words, by the other passage, "Let the elders that rule well be counted worthy of double honour, especially they who labour in the word and doctrine; for the Scripture saith, Thou shalt not muzzle the ox that treadeth out the corn."\* How beautifully is this large lesson of charity and justice developed out of what might seem a very trivial and unimportant precept! "Doth God take care for oxen?" Certainly He does, but He takes care

\* 1 Tim. v. 17, 18.

for man much more. When He tells us that it is a duty to be considerate of the former, He reminds us that it is a still more urgent duty to feel sympathy for the latter. It is our Lord's argument, "Not a sparrow falls to the ground without your Father: ye are of more value than many sparrows;"* and again, "Which of you shall have a sheep fallen into a pit on the Sabbath and will not lift it out? How much is a man better than a sheep?"† By thus inculcating the duty of considerately caring for dumb animals, the Jewish Law really enforces the general principle, the wider duty, which embraces all things, "both great and small." Our poet's words come here irresistibly into the mind,—

* Matt. x. 29, 31.      † Matt. xii. 11, 12.

> "The dear God who loveth us
> He made and loveth all."

And indeed this considerate care in the minor instance is itself a training for humanity and kindness in reference to the greater. Such a suggestion as that of this little precept in the Pentateuch, furnished to a thoughtful, devout, and feeling mind, spreads out into a thousand instances, and finds its opportunities in all the relations of life, and especially those relations where service on our behalf has established a claim to our gratitude.

## IV.

## GREEK GAMES.

THE four short essays in which I am inviting attention to four of St Paul's favourite metaphors, do not by any means exhaust the characteristic imagery of that Apostle; and in order to give a better completeness to the series, it may be useful to prefix to this last essay a few general remarks on the whole subject.

A single example, selected out of those which have previously been given, may (though at the risk of some repetition) conveniently introduce these general remarks. St Paul, in writing his first Epistle to the Corinthians, says to them, as we have seen,* "Ye are God's building." These simple words are like the striking of a key-note. There follows immediately the full swell of a familiar passage,† with all its melodious rhythm, and its intricate verbal and moral harmonies. There is no need to occupy ourselves again with the religious meanings of the passage. Attention is simply directed to the characteristic nature of the allegory. If we place ourselves at Ephesus, where the letter was written, or at Corinth, where the letter was received, and mark the evident and outward characteristics of such places, we see at once the

* See p. 78.    † 1 Cor. iii. 9-15.

significance of the language. Conspicuous in these cities were vast public buildings, such as the Temple of Diana at Ephesus,* and similar edifices at Corinth—strong, firm, and magnificent, with columns and slabs of marble, porphyry, and granite—" precious stones "—and richly completed with metallic decorations—" gold and silver." But close beside them were the hovels of the poor, with a sharpness of contrast to which we are not accustomed, but which we can in some degree set before our minds by imagining some of our great public edifices to be densely surrounded by an accumulation of wretched villages, with huts hastily run up with "wood," the interstices filled with "hay," and the roof thatched with

* See Acts xix. 27.

"stubble." And now suppose a fire to take place in such a scene, and you have immediately the simple outward image on which the Apostle's manifold parable rests. All these wretched hovels, so cheaply, so carelessly built, would be burnt up; and all that could be hoped for to the poor man himself, in any one of them, would be a bare personal escape through the flames. The great building, on the other hand, might be scorched and blackened, but it would stand steady and erect, and exhibit still all the proofs of patient working in the quarry, of good and solid masonry, and of rich and elaborate ornament. In listening to expositions of this passage, we often find that this plain and simple way of looking at it has never occurred to the expositor, and we are presented with the unreal and grotesque image of a rubbish-heap, consisting of sticks and straw, and containing also some contents of a jeweller's shop, diamonds, rubies, and garnets. This is not the style in which St Paul would be likely to write to educated men. And misconceptions of such a kind arise from this, that men, in interpreting Scripture, so often look only at the words and not at the things; so often forget that every writer in the Bible drew his illustrations from the circumstances with which he was surrounded, and especially those circumstances which were most in harmony with the temperament of mind which the Holy Ghost, in that particular case, consecrated and employed.

The general notion, then, of these essays is

this, that in order to enter into the full force of St Paul's writings, it is needful to have, not only that clear apprehension of the meaning of his words, which we obtain through our exact study of Greek literature, but also that apprehension of the familiar sights and sounds, customs and institutions, surrounding him, which is furnished by our knowledge of history and antiquities, science and art; and further, to consider carefully what portions of that outward environment he most employs by preference or habit in the inculcation of religious truth. In studying the Bible, the dictionary of things is almost as important as the dictionary of words; and St Paul's writings are no exception to this rule, but one of its best exemplifications.

As to his own temperament and predilection,

we may again revert to a remark which was made before,* that his metaphors are usually drawn, not from the operations and phenomena of the natural world, but from the activities and the outward manifestations of human life. In this respect, St Paul's illustrative language has already been contrasted with that of St James. "The vapour, the fierce wind, the fountain, beasts and birds and serpents, the flower of the grass, the wave of the sea, the early and latter rain, the sun risen with a burning heat,"†—these are like the figures of the ancient prophets. There is more imagery of this kind, I think, in the one short Epistle of St James, than in all the speeches and letters of St Paul put together. The address to the

* Page 94.   † James iv. 14; iii. 4, 7, 11, 12 : i. 6, 10, 11; v. 7.

idolaters of Lystra,* country-people as they were in a rude and remote district, if it is an exception at all, is exactly that kind of exception which makes the general rule more palpably evident.

St Paul's favourite figures are undoubtedly taken from the midst of the busiest human society. Four of these have been selected for careful examination, and we are now proceeding to consider the fourth. But others of the same general type might easily have been added to the list; and again, for the sake of completeness, it may be desirable to name two or three instances. Thus, first, how large a portion of St Paul's attention is given to *money-matters!* How often are his images

* Acts xiv. 15–17.

drawn from the market! To take only three instances:—"Owe no man anything, but to love one another."* It would be impossible, perhaps, by the use of any other illustration, to express with equal force all that this sentence implies. Again, in the phrase, "Redeem the time,"† what is really said is this, "Buy out of the market what you may never buy so cheap again; use the opportunity while you have it, and use it thoroughly." So again, his reference to the *law courts* and the administration of justice, even when he is arguing points of theology, is an instance which strikes us forcibly. An interesting question arises, whether in such passages he refers mainly to Jewish law or to Roman law, especially when

* Rom. xiii. 8. † Eph. v. 16; Col. iv. 5.

the allusion is to marriage\* and the making of wills;† but in either case his consistency is preserved as regards the characteristic nature of his imagery. A third instance is that of *slavery*, as was almost inevitable for such a writer at this period of history. In the ancient world, war and slavery ran into one another; and throughout the Roman Empire the whole of society was made up of the contrasts of "bond" and "free,"‡ with the freedmen (and such, probably, were St Paul's own ancestors) intermediate between the two. Hence, when speaking of the most momentous alternatives in the condition of the soul, his language is drawn from the experience of slaves. The

---

\* Rom. vii. 3, 4.   † Gal. iii. 15; iv. 1.
‡ 1 Cor. xii. 13; Gal. iii. 28; Col. iii. 11.

great and decisive change is expressed thus:— "Being emancipated from that cruel master, Sin, ye are now the happy slaves of a good master, God."* But it is time to proceed without delay to our proper subject. The imagery to which our special consideration is to be given now is the most animated of all, being derived from the lively and exciting *games of the Greeks.*

There is an obvious reason why images of this kind should have been very familiar to St Paul's thoughts, and why, when made the vehicles of instruction, they should have been very helpful to his converts. Wherever he was residing, at Corinth, at Athens, and in all places where a Greek population was predominant,

* Rom. vi. 18, 22. See vii. 23; viii. 21.

(and this was, in fact, over the whole of the Levant,) the athletic games of the Greeks came before his notice, as a subject which caused the most engrossing and universal interest. The *Gymnasium*, or place of training, and the *Stadium*, or ground for running, were among the most conspicuous and most frequented spots in the architecture and embellishment of the cities. Of many of them the remains can still be traced. Wrestling, boxing, and especially foot-races, with all the preliminary training, with the assembled and applauding multitudes while the contest was going on, with the formality of the heralds and the strict observance of the rules, with the umpires and prizes and eager congratulations at the close, with the poems which perpetuated great victories like heir-looms through successive generations,—these things were almost a religion among the Greeks, and they caused an enthusiasm which we ourselves can hardly understand, though it does happen that in our day athletic sports are a fancy and a fashion, and really in some cases, it would seem, almost a religion.

I said, especially the foot-race. This was pre-eminently the struggle which caused the most eager interest in that age and in those countries. And this is pre-eminently the image which seems to come obviously to the Apostle, when he employs comparisons of this kind. We find instances in the book of Acts. Thus, when he is preaching one of his great missionary sermons at Antioch in Pisidia, and has occasion to mention John the Baptist, he speaks of him as "*fulfilling his course,*"* which literally means, "running the race he had to run;" and this lively expression is evidently a fitting representation of that career, which did not last very long, but was very energetic while it lasted. So in addressing the elders at Miletus, and speaking of himself, and alluding with deep feeling to the "bonds and afflictions" which awaited him, he says: "None of these things move me, neither count I my life dear unto myself, that I may *finish my course* with joy." † He knows that his course requires a vigorous effort—he feels that there are many things to dissuade him from it and to cause him to turn aside—but he braces himself up, like a runner, for the struggle, throws himself into it with all his force and

---

\* Acts xiii. 25. † Acts xx. 24.

spirit, and thinks of the joy and exultation which await him at the close.

Similar, and very frequently, is his language in the Epistles. It is well worth our while to observe how generally and variously this figure is distributed through them. Some phrases of this kind must appear strange to those who do not consider the context of circumstances by which the Apostle was surrounded. Thus, to take as our guide the same English word which we have observed in the Acts: "Pray for us," he says to the Thessalonians, "that the word of the Lord may have *free course* and be glorified."\* Here the Gospel itself is the runner, for which he desires a race that shall be vigorous, rapid, free from obstacles, and triumphant

\* 2 Thess. iii. 1.

at the end. Again, to turn to most pathetic language having reference to himself, he writes to Timothy, "I have fought the good fight: I have finished *my course:* I have kept the faith : henceforth there is laid up for me the crown of righteousness, which the Lord, the righteous judge, shall give me at that day."\* We must be careful here to give the right meaning to the word "fight." This term has nothing to do with war. It denotes an *athletic* contest. And the particular kind of athletic contest, which he specifies in his customary way, is the foot-race. But now he is writing near the close of life. The race is nearly run, the struggle is all but over, he is weary, as it were, and panting with the effort, but he is successful, the crown is in

\* 2 Tim. iv. 7, 8.

sight, and the judge, the "righteous" judge, who cannot make a mistake, is there, ready to place that bright wreath upon his head.

And as with the word "course," so with the verb that corresponds with it.* "It is not of him that willeth, nor of him that *runneth*," says St Paul in an argument,† which turns all our confidence towards Him who "hath compassion" and "showeth mercy." His anxiety regarding the success of his own Apostolic work, is expressed by the same image in two very different Epistles, written at widely-separated points of time. He tells the Galatians that at an early period he negotiated very carefully at

---

\* In 2 Thess. iii. 1, the margin has "run." No use is here made of Heb. xii. 1, simply because in these essays it is not desirable absolutely to assume the Pauline authorship of that Epistle. † Rom. ix. 15, 16.

Jerusalem, "lest by any means he *should run* or *had run* in vain;"* and writing long afterwards from Rome to the Philippians, he expresses his desire that they may be consistent, in order that he himself "may rejoice in the day of Christ, that he has not *run* in vain."† And the metaphor which he applies to the progress of the Gospel committed to him, he applies also to the practical consistency and progress of those who had learnt the truth from him. "Ye did *run* well," he says to some, who had grievously failed and fallen: "who hath hindered you, that ye should not obey the truth?"‡ "Ye were running the Christian race successfully and well: who put these obstacles in your way, which have thrown you down, and brought

* Gal. ii. 2.   † Phil. ii. 16.   ‡ Gal. v. 7.

you to shame?" The whole language, as read in the original Greek, is far more easily recognised as applicable to the foot-race, than can possibly be perceived in the English version.

Thus we see that both direct and indirect advantages may be gained, by pursuing a narrow line of thought suggested by mere words. We here perceive the harmony of St Paul's language in his speeches and his letters, and lay hold on one of the small collateral proofs of the genuine and honest character both of the Acts and the Epistles. We are very far, however, as yet from having mentioned all instances of the use of such metaphors in these latter documents; and perhaps their use, in fact, strikes us all the more, when the actual words, to which our attention has hitherto been given, are not employed. Thus, when St Paul says to Timothy, "Exercise thyself unto godliness,"* the word he employs is most distinctly taken from the training and practising for *gymnastic* contests. And then he adds: "Bodily exercise profiteth little, but godliness is profitable unto all things, having the promise of the life that now is, and of that which is to come"†—a passage often misinterpreted. It is, in fact, frequently distorted in two ways. The "bodily exercise" is taken to mean religious asceticism, and the contrast is understood to lie between this and some supposed "godliness" not connected with bodily self-denial; whereas the comparison is simply between the training of the body for the games, and the training of the

* 1 Tim. iv. 7. † Ver. 8.

whole man, body, soul, and spirit, in the life of religion. And this helps us to avoid the other mistake, which is often committed in the interpretation of the passage. It would be a strange thing, if St Paul were to urge his disciple to the practice of a strict religious training of his character, by any promise relating chiefly to this life. He does nothing of the kind. He points out that, if the athletes will do so much for a reward which is merely of this world, we ought to do much under the influence of a promise which relates not merely to this world, but also to the next. God has indeed a blessing for this world, as the blessing of Esau, but His highest blessing is for the next world, even as the blessing of Jacob. It is as if St Paul said to Timothy, (and we could well imagine that such recollections of the past were in his mind as he wrote,) "My son Timothy, thou rememberest how, when we were at Corinth,* with our brother Silas, and Crispus, the ruler of the synagogue, we watched the athletes training for the games; young men of noble forms, eager and active, patient and persevering. It was a foolish toil, for a worthless reward. But we may learn a serviceable lesson from them. The children of this world are in their generation more diligent than the children of light. Train thyself —thy religious character—with the like eagerness and activity, patience and perseverance. Thy reward is not only earthly, but heavenly." And similar trains of thought might be followed in reference to other phrases, where not ob-

* Acts xviii. 5, 8.

viously at first sight, but still really, images from the games are imbedded in the context of the Epistles. Thus, when he says that he himself has spoken the Gospel of God "with much contention," * or that others have been "striving fervently" † in intercessory prayer, or when he tells Timothy to "fight the good fight of faith," ‡ the metaphor is really *agonistic*, though the variations in the English version conceal the fact. But we must turn now to more copious passages, where the agonistic allegory is presented in its most animated form.

In the Epistle to the Philippians St Paul writes thus: "Not as though I had already attained, either were already perfect—but I follow after. This one thing I do, forgetting those

---

\* 1 Thess. ii. 2.      † Col. iv. 12.      ‡ 1 Tim. vi. 12.

things which are behind, and reaching forth unto those things which are before, I press toward the mark for the prize of the high calling of God in Christ Jesus."* Was there ever a more vigorous picture of a runner in earnest? Here is the eager pressing towards a definite end in view—the feeling that nothing else is to be thought of for the present—the determination that nothing shall interfere with the matter in hand;—and at the same time, with this strong effort of the will, there is the utmost alacrity and activity of movement. Here is no looking back, no thought of giving up the struggle. The whole energy of mind and body is bent upon success; and till success is achieved, nothing is done. It would be easy to dwell on

* Phil. iii. 12-14.

these points at greater length; but really the best commentary on the passage is supplied by the familiar facts of a well contested foot-race.

And there is yet a still more copious and lively instance of the same kind of illustration. As in the discussions of the other metaphors, some one passage was selected as furnishing the best sample, and as containing in fact the main basis for the discussion, so here we turn naturally to some verses in the ninth chapter of the First Epistle to the Corinthians: " Know ye not that they which run in a race, run all, but one obtaineth the prize? So run, that ye may obtain. And every man that striveth for the mastery is temperate in all things. Now they do it that they may obtain a fading crown; but we an unfading. I therefore so run, not as uncertainly; so fight I, not as one that beateth the air: but I keep under my body, and bring it into subjection; lest that by any means, when I have preached to others, I myself should be a castaway."* It may perhaps be a help towards our entering fully into the spiritual meaning of this passage, if we try to associate one practical topic with each one of the four verses.

And the topic which we may associate with the first of the verses is this: the *earnestness of purpose* that is essential to the Christian's career. "Know ye not that they which run in a race, run all, but one receiveth the prize? So run, that ye may obtain." St Paul appeals to the *experience* of the Corinthians. There was nothing with which they were better acquainted

* 1 Cor. ix. 24-27.

than these famous foot-races. Their own games near their own city were among the most celebrated in the world. They "knew" well that each race was eagerly contested, and that "one" obtained the prize. But at this point we must mark a difference. In that race there was competition; and because there was competition, each runner was in earnest. In the Christian race there is no competition. The prize is within the reach of all. But then each runner must be as much in earnest as though there were competition and only one prize. And this is what the Apostle expresses. He does not say (as I understand his words) "run *so—in such a way—as to* obtain,"—but, "run *so—as those runners run—in order that* ye may obtain." In their case there is rivalry, and therefore they are in earnest. In your case there is no rivalry; but their earnestness of purpose is an example to you.

And certainly no pattern of earnestness can be a more forcible example, than the earnestness that arises from eager competition. "Run in the Christian race as the athlete in the foot-race runs." All his nerves and sinews are strung up for the effort he is making. Nothing else is thought of; and as the distance between his feet and the winning-post diminishes, he does not flag, but throws more and more exertion into the movement of his limbs. Whatever strength and elasticity he can summon up, whatever struggling remainder of his short and failing breath he can muster, all may be wanted at the very last moment. And what a contrast this is to our dull and languid Christianity! We go and take our place in the course as though the prize could be won without any running at all, or as if there were no prize worth running for. We dream and loiter and fold our arms; we turn aside to look at every object of passing interest; or if we did begin with some vigour, all the zest and warmth of the struggle grows feebler and fainter when it ought to become more animated, and, like the Galatians, we care little what hindrances occur to stop our course, and to risk a dishonourable fall. Earnestness of purpose is what we want, and there is no picture of earnestness more forcible than that which is drawn from the ardour of competition.

But now we pass to the next verse—"Every man that striveth for the mastery is temperate in all things;" and the lesson is pointed by a contrast—"They do it to obtain a corruptible crown, but we an incorruptible." The successful athlete in the Greek foot-race received for his prize a crown of green leaves, placed by the judge upon his head. In itself it was of no value; but it was the mark of victory. The winning of this crown was sung in poetry: it was the subject of pride and congratulation to the city from which the successful runner came; and it was the ground of boasting for long generations afterwards in his family. For the winning of this, exertions were made involving the utmost patience and self-denial, and no waste of strength and activity was thought too great if only it could be secured. And yet it was only a corruptible, a fading crown. 'Its beauty passed away sooner than the beauty of those leaves which are stripped off from our trees by the winds of November. And indeed *all* human glory is a fading crown. It *must* wither and die in the end. Yet what trouble men take to obtain it! And what an example in this respect is the eager lover of glory to the Christian! His crown can never fade. To lose that crown, as it certainly may be lost, by neglect, by indolence, by turning out of the right course, by falling headlong over temptations that lie before our very feet, this is surely the strangest and most unaccountable folly; while to win it is worth far more, ten thousand times, than all the toil of the most faithful servant of Christ, all the torture of the most suffering martyr.

This verse, however, points not to suffering, but to self-restraint, which self-restraint is itself a blessing; and the topic which we may associate with these words in the Apostle's comparison might be expressed thus—*self-restraint inspired by hope.* It is often worth a man's while to give up something which he values for the sake of some higher good in prospect. This is what was done in the Greek athletic sports when the competitors were under training; and so indeed it is now, sometimes to an absurd extent, in English athletic sports. Classical authors furnish us with materials, by help of which we might, if it were necessary, describe the strict discipline to which these young Greeks were subjected under the trainer—the diet, the exercise, the hard life, the fixed hours, the peremptory abstinence from everything likely to hinder the end in view. It is the *example* to the *Christian* presented by this discipline which is the point before us. Nor is this the only place where the same Apostle makes a similar reference. In writing another of his Epistles, he says, "If a man also strive for masteries, yet is he not crowned, except he strive lawfully;"\* *i.e.*, he cannot obtain the prize unless he complies with the regulations; and these regulations included, among other things, very strict and systematic methods of discipline and training. And the gospel strife with earthly sin for a heavenly prize has likewise its strict regulations. There is a preparatory discipline and training to which the Christian must be subjected before he

\* 2 Tim. ii. 5.

can be fit to enter on his reward. The discipline, however, is, as was said before, itself a blessing. The training is a training for happiness. The Apostle expresses it thus—"temperance in all things;" the habit of self-restraint running through the whole life; a check placed, not only on the passions, but on the words; moderation strictly practised in food and in sleep; those eager desires for amusement and novelty kept in control; so that the man is always master of himself. Thus under God's grace that character is formed, which commands respect and exerts influence in this life, and is prepared to enter on the future life, where no sin and folly disturb the balance of the purified soul. It is the hope of that life which furnishes the motive for self-restraint, just as the hope of victory in the foot-race gives the athlete patience to submit to all the discipline and training required by the rules.

"I therefore so run, not as uncertainly; so fight I, not as one that beateth the air," is the next of the Apostle's sentences. *Definiteness of aim*, then, in the Christian's race and contest, is our next topic. And it will be observed that St Paul presents this subject under two images, one drawn from running, the other from boxing. The foot-race was, as I have said, the most popular athletic contest among the Greeks; and it supplied to the Apostle his favourite comparison, in connexion with subjects of this class. But the *pugilistic* contest was also constant and familiar at the public games, and he combines this contest with the other in illustration of the point which is now before us. Not only does the Christian act with earnestness of purpose, not only is he encouraged to practise self-restraint, but he is definite in his aims. And in two ways he is definite. He has a distinct view of the objects of his desire, and a distinct view of the enemies against which he must contend.

"I so run, not as uncertainly." A man who does not know his own mind is seldom successful. That is a very unhappy temperament which is easily turned this way and that, and which always yields to the latest influence, is always persuaded by the last new argument. Such a man is continually in the hands of others. He is never his own master. He never does anything well. And there is another very unhappy habit of mind: when a man does not go direct to his point—when he tries experiments on the right and on the left—when he loses time by hesitation, or follows circuitous methods, whereas the straightforward course is always the best. They are both opposed to the true dignity of Christian principle. The disciple of Christ should be known as a simple-hearted man. His eye is single. He has one great object before him. His desire is to be like Christ, to prepare for spending eternity with that Blessed Master, and meanwhile to honour Him by doing good to all around him. And nothing could express this in a more lively manner than the comparison with the runner in a race. Direct—with the goal straight before him—with his whole frame vigorously moving that way—moving, too, by the shortest path—such is his course. Let such be our course. "Forgetting the things that are behind, and reaching forward to the things that are before, let us press toward the mark of the prize of our high calling."

But still, while we have a course to run, we have also enemies to fight; and, to express this, another metaphor is appropriate—"So fight I, not as one that beateth the air." St Paul passes here from the runner to the boxer, and, drawing a comparison from this source, he points out that the Christian has very definite antagonists. With the pugilist it is no mere striking for striking's sake, no mere pastime, no dealing of blows in the air for the exercise of the muscles. When the Corinthians or Athenians or Ephesians came in crowds to see their favourite athlete engaged in this contest, it was no showy and unmeaning attitudes that they came to witness, but the vigilant and most active employment of hand and eye for the purpose of victory over an opponent equally active and vigilant. And the best application which we can make for ourselves of this apostolic comparison is this—that we must be on the alert against our besetting sins—that we must keep our attention fixed upon them, and deal our blows steadily against them. Now, in order to do this, we must first know what our besetting sins really are. This is a most serious subject. It is not sin in general that we have to contend against, not the sins of our neighbours, not the sins which we have no temptation to commit, but "the sin which doth so easily beset us."\* What is that sin? Has the reader discovered his besetting sin? If not—this is not the place for dogmatising on spiritual things—but it may well be doubted whether it is possible for us to be saved at all, unless we have found out our besetting sin.

Now let us consider the last of these four emphatic verses: "I keep under my body, and bring it into subjection: lest that by any means, when I have preached unto others, I myself should be a castaway." The image of the pugilist is still continued here; and we have to observe, first, *what* the Apostle does, and, secondly, *why* he does it. He resists his carnal nature, systematically attacks it, and perseveres till he has subdued it; and this he does under

---

\* Heb. xii. 1.

the influence of a salutary fear, lest, whilst he has been made a blessing to others, he himself should fail to obtain the reward. The topic then suggested by this part of the passage might be expressed thus: *persevering effort inspired by fear.*

The simple fact of St Paul using this image at all is a very grave fact. This pugilistic encounter was no mere light and languid amusement. Very often it was a matter of life and death. And certainly there is something very revolting in the thought of such a combat (whether in Ancient Greece or in Modern England) being made an entertainment for a crowd of spectators. But these Corinthians, Ephesians, and Athenians, were heathens, and whatever we may feel on this subject does not affect the strong significance of the Apostle's comparison. It is the intense reality of the struggle which constitutes the point of resemblance. Those heavy blows, dealt by one combatant with tremendous force upon the other, are taken to signify the resolute and incessant warfare which the Christian maintains with whatever is sinful in his human nature. These fleshly inclinations are determined to give *him* no rest, and he is determined to give *them* no rest: and he perseveres till the blows of this opponent become weak and faint, and he is master of the field. This is a very serious picture of the Christian life in one of its aspects: and it shows it to be very different from what it is sometimes supposed to be—a mere habit of passive acquiescence in certain opinions—a mere decorous compliance with certain rules of society—a mere receiving of impressions from without, unaccompanied by any spring of resolute energy from within.

But it is quite as important, and even more important, to observe the *motive* of the Apostle in this energetic and vigilant resistance. His persevering effort is inspired by *fear*. "I keep under my body, and bring it into subjection: lest that by any means, when I have preached unto others, I myself should be a castaway." "*Lest*"—never was a little word more weighty in any sentence; and the writer makes it more emphatic, by the addition of "*by any means.*" Could there be a more solemn admonition of danger? Here is this great Apostle, to whom the establishment of Christianity in the world is due more than to any one else, telling us that he carried on a watchful and vigorous warfare against his fleshly nature, *for fear lest*, in the midst of all these ministrations, he himself should lose his reward. Well, then, may we fear for ourselves; and, most of all, those amongst us who are actively endeavouring to do spiritual good to others. What thought can go with greater power into the very depths of the conscience than this : "God may be using me for the spiritual good of others, and yet my own heart may not be right; my own soul may not be safe, through the mysterious power of sin in my fleshly nature : I may be falling away farther from God, even while I am drawing others nearer to Him ?" It is of course obvious that we are here brought into contact with the doctrines of predestination and election, and that a difficulty arises when such a passage as this is compared with passages supporting these doctrines. It is easy to range texts on both sides of such a controversy as that, and not easy to reconcile them, except by making one set of texts give way to another. And this we have no right to do. With other parts of Scripture before us, we might meditate with advantage on the sweet comfort which is derived from the conviction that those who have placed their souls in the care of Christ are safe, and that no one can pluck them out of that Saviour's hands. But that is not our subject now. We must take the Bible as we find it. St Paul does most distinctly tell us in this place that *with him* the fear of being "a castaway" was a commanding motive. Hope and fear are the two poles of the Christian's life; and certainly fear has a very conspicuous place in Holy Scriptures. "Be not high-minded, but *fear*." "Pass the time of your sojourning here in *fear*." "Let him that thinketh he standeth *take heed* lest he fall." \*

The general subject of St Paul's habit of taking metaphorical language from the athletic games is by no means yet exhausted. Even in the context which we have been examining at considerable length, there is at least one other agonistic allusion, which might easily escape notice. When St Paul speaks in this passage of "having preached to others," the true rendering is, "having been *a herald* to others." And the reference is to that officer in the concourse at the games, whose business it was, with

\* Rom. xi. 20; 1 Pet. i. 17; 1 Cor. x. 12.

his voice, or with a trumpet, to summon the competitors to the exciting struggle. Much more, too, might be said on various points of detail, which have been only lightly touched, such as the training,* the rules,† the judge,‡ the prize,§ the attending spectators, ‖ and the jubilant joy ¶ with which the victor was received at the close of the race. But it is now time to lay the subject aside; and this short series of papers on St Paul's illustrative language may be briefly concluded by two reflections, one of which has reference to the Apostle himself, the other to the Bible at large.

It is impossible not to feel, in pursuing such studies as these, that we have not merely St

---

\* 1 Cor. ix. 25 ; 1 Tim. iv. 7, 8.    † 2 Tim. ii. 5.    ‡ 2 Tim. iv. 8.
§ 1 Cor. ix. 24 ; Phil. iii. 14.    ‖ 1 Cor. iv. 9.    ¶ Acts xx. 24.

Paul's instruction and exhortation, but his personal example, before us. We always feel that we should like to know something of the character of a man who produced such wonderful effects in the world as the Apostle Paul. And certainly, we have no lack of materials for forming a judgment on this subject. Among other things, we have his customary language. A man's customary language (at least if he is a man of mark) generally shows something of his character; and perhaps especially the language which he uses in his letters. For in letter-writing we are free from the disturbing influences of conversation, while yet the personal element is strongly present. Four groups of St Paul's favourite similes have been before our attention, and perhaps each of them might furnish a suggestion in regard to his character. Thus, in his architectural imagery we might be reminded of his steady adherence to first principles, and of his constructive ability (under God's Spirit) in regard both to doctrine and the Church; while his illustrations drawn from agriculture seem to present him before us in his sympathising care for the spiritual growth of his converts and his reliance on the exercise of God's beneficent power. But perhaps it is more easy to make this use of the metaphors which he draws from Roman soldiers and Greek games. We can hardly be mistaken in believing that by combining them together we obtain an approximate picture of the man. In both cases his references to such subjects are copious, natural, and customary. From this we should conclude that there was something of the Soldier and the Athlete in his moral and religious constitution. And so in truth it was. He had much of what we should call tenacity of character—a great power of elastic recovery, when he was beaten back by opposition—a strong will, not deterred by difficulties—and at the same time a remarkable alacrity and versatility and readiness of resource. We know this to have been the case, from the facts of his life; but we see it also in the imagery which he is in the habit of borrowing from the Roman Soldiers and the Greek Games.

As to Scripture in general, the remark which suggests itself in conclusion is this, that the careful student can in every part of it enter upon large and precious trains of thought, and can find a germinating power even in what seem to be its secondary portions. In these short essays we have been following very narrow paths through a very limited portion of God's Word; and yet we have found a good deal to interest and instruct us. It is a great proof of the endless variety and richness of the Bible, if we can gain so much by merely pursuing the course of a peculiar word or a characteristic metaphor. God's Word is like God's World, very varied, very rich, very beautiful. You never know when you have exhausted all its secrets. The Bible, like Nature, has something for every class of mind. As in the phenomena around us there are resources and invitations both for science and for poetry, so does God's Revelation furnish materials both for exact theological definition and for the free play of devout thought and feeling. Look at the Bible in a new light, and you straightway see some new charm. This is true, even in regard to very minute particulars. The view from a commanding Alpine summit, which has been climbed by great labour, and where half a kingdom is spread before you, is very glorious and not to be forgotten: but the quiet footpath along the slopes of the lower eminences may also be full of beauty at every turn. And such has been our modest course in these essays. It is something to have obtained a deeper conviction than before of the inexhaustible charms and advantages of even the byways of Scripture.

*Ballantyne & Company, Printers, Edinburgh.*